What Can the Tarot

On its own, Tarot is neutral, except perhaps in one regard. There seems to be an inherent message of balance in the cards themselves. Over and over, the cards suggest that it is the middle way that we should seek, that extremes can be useful, but that living in an extreme state for a prolonged time is not healthy. Over and over, the cards show a central figure sitting or standing between two extremes: a white or black pillar, a man or woman, a pair of sphinxes, twin towers, and more. Over and over, masculine is balanced with feminine, action is balanced with inaction, solar is balanced with lunar, light is balanced with dark, and Tarot makes no judgments against male or female, action or inaction, solar or lunar, light or dark. The only judgment seems to be that both are needed, both are necessary, both are valuable.

Tarot teaches us not only this lesson about the duality of life; it also teaches us the lesson of balance with the four classic elements of air, fire, water, and earth. Water is not better than fire, nor earth than air. All four elements are necessary. All four have valuable lessons for us. All four have gifts and challenges for us.

Therefore, if a person were just to look at the deck of Tarot cards, over and over and over, I believe that he or she would learn valuable lessons about the nature of life and about how to live so that his or her life would be a vital life of growth and exploration. It is with this belief that I began to write exercises using the Tarot for self-discovery.

—Nina Lee Braden

About the Author

Nina Lee Braden, a Tarot reader and astrologer, is a Certified Tarot Instructor with the Tarot Certification Board, and a member of the American Tarot Association. She is the webmaster of the award-winning website, Moonstruck (at http://www.ninalee.com), which features original articles on Tarot, astrology, soulmates, alternative health, and other topics. She is also on the editorial board of the *Tarot Journal*, speaks on Tarot, astrology, and soulmates at many regional conferences, and has presented Tarot for Self Discovery at ATA conferences in 2000 and 2001. She has also taught Tarot at the Southeastern Unitarian Universalist Summer Institute and at Womongathering.

Nina Lee is a college English teacher, with a master's degree in that subject. In addition to being a Tarot reader and astrologer, she is a freelance copy editor. She is a lifelong resident of Tennessee.

To Write to the Author

If you wish to contact the author or would like more information about this book, please write to the author in care of Llewellyn Worldwide and we will forward your request. Both the author and publisher appreciate hearing from you and learning of your enjoyment of this book. Llewellyn Worldwide cannot guarantee that every letter written to the author will be answered, but all will be forwarded. Please write to:

Nina Lee Braden
℅ Llewellyn Worldwide
P.O. Box 64383, Dept. 0-7387-0170-X
St. Paul, MN 55164-0383, U.S.A.

Please include a self-addressed, stamped envelope with your letter.
If outside the U.S.A., enclose international postal coupons.

Many of Llewellyn's authors have websites with additional information and resources. For more information, please visit our website at www.llewellyn.com.

Special Topics in Tarot

TAROT
FOR SELF DISCOVERY

NINA LEE BRADEN

with

INTRODUCTION BY MARY K. GREER

2002
Llewellyn Publications
St. Paul, Minnesota 64383-0383, U.S.A.

FIRST EDITION
First Printing, 2002

Cover art © 2001 by Brian Williams, background image © 2001 Photodisc
Cover design by Kevin R. Brown
Editing and interior design by Connie Hill

Library of Congress Cataloging-in-Publication Data
Braden, Nina Lee
    Tarot for self discovery / Nina Lee Braden : with foreword by Mary K. Greer.
  — 1st ed.
    p.   cm.
    Includes bibliographical references.
    ISBN 0–7387-0170-X (pbk)
  1. Tarot.   I. Title.

BF1879.T2 B73   2002
133.3'2424—dc21   2002022242

Llewellyn Publications
A Division of Llewellyn Worldwide, Ltd.
P.O. Box 64383, Dept. 0-7387-0170-X
St. Paul, MN 55164-0383, U.S.A.
http://www.llewellyn.com

Printed in the United States of America on recycled paper

Table of Contents

Acknowledgments

No book is written in a vacuum, and certainly not this one. I have read many books and learned from many teachers. I take my inspiration from life, and many times I do not remember or even know my original source of inspiration.

That said, there are certain debts of gratitude that are notable and that need to be expressed. First and foremost, I am thankful to Mary Greer and Rachel Pollack. Their works on Tarot constitute the bedrock of all that I know and do in Tarot. Their guiding light has oftentimes shown me the way. I admire them tremendously and consider myself extremely fortunate to have studied with them at the Omega Institute.

For inspiration for individual exercises, I wish to thank Toni Norman, Valerie Behi, and the members of my former e-mail list: Tarot of Self Discovery. I also wish to thank Valerie for sharing some of these exercises with her students and allowing me to share her interaction with one of her students in the sample exercises on these pages.

For support and encouragement, I wish to thank Barbara Moore at Llewellyn and John Gilbert of the American Tarot Association. Both of them took chances by giving me opportunities, and I am grateful.

Many friends have for years urged me to write a book on Tarot, despite my protests that I had nothing new to say: Debra Butler, Kathy Tallent, Debbie Duckett, Nancy Leonard, Manderley Swain, Dee Ashe, Sherry Peruzzi,

Diane Wilkes, Natalie Bradley, Ellie Miller, Kate McMurry, Lady Rowena, Lawrence and Lydia Moore, Patsy Haggerty, Marla Franks, and Phyllis Vega.

My family has been extremely enthusiastic about this book, even while simultaneously providing unlimited distractions that kept me away from the keyboard. My husband, Mike Willis; my daughters, Mary Frances Milligan and Katherine Milligan; and my stepson, Brook Willis—all have cheered me on as I worked on this project.

foreword

I am so pleased to introduce *Tarot for Self Discovery* as one of the first books in Llewellyn's new series of "Special Topics in Tarot." It is a perfect example of a work that, while it can be used by a Tarot novice, has been specifically designed for those who already know Tarot's value as a source of insight and inspiration. *Tarot for Self Discovery* doesn't set out to teach you how to read the cards, nor does it give you meanings to memorize. In no way does it suggest, however, that these are not important. What Nina Lee Braden offers is an additional, innovative use of the Tarot, specifically for self-empowerment and change. She encourages you to study with teachers and other books.

Read this book with your Tarot deck and journal in hand. Stop and do the exercises and you are likely to learn quite a bit about Tarot, but even more about yourself. Do the "concrete steps" and I guarantee you'll move through personal limitations and discover hidden potentials. It's a little scary, but also very exciting. Processes like those found here are what have given me my deepest joys and greatest satisfaction with the cards. They offer an invigorating way of discovering both depth and new directions in your Tarot practice, but most of all, they provide you with experiences and knowledge you will never forget. The figures on the cards will speak to you, teach you, move through you.

Exercises like "Happy Feet" turn the deck into a playful tool kit with which you construct a mood, renovate spirits, and build experiences to your own liking. Others like "Lost in a Wasteland" or "Unnamed Exercise (Grief)" reveal tough truths and help you face pain. As Nina Lee makes so clear, self-discovery is about seeing our faults and flaws; balancing denial and self-blame; and discerning blessings, gifts, and strengths. Tarot is our tool, and self-discovery our goal.

Most of the time you will be choosing cards in an unusual way—which I pride myself on pioneering in *Tarot for Your Self*. You will be choosing cards by looking through a deck faceup, instead of getting Dame Fortune's "luck of the draw." As Nina Lee explains, choosing cards faceup empowers you to examine your psyche; facedown shows you your fate. Part of the fun is mixing and matching these two perspectives. The cards can mean anything you want them to mean, yet your responses to them, guided by Nina Lee's acute questions, will surprise and enlighten.

Many of the exercises are closer to true magic than what you will find in books of formulaic spells and enchantments. Magical rituals are *symbols in action* that bring about transformation and change in accord with will. That is exactly what you will find here.

I hope you will enjoy the entire series of "Special Topics in Tarot" as they are designed to take our knowledge and uses of the cards where no one has gone before.

Mary K. Greer
Author of *Tarot for Your Self* and
The Complete Book of Tarot Reversals
January 15, 2002

ONE

WHAT IS TAROT FOR SELF-DISCOVERY?

According to the best current historical assessment, Tarot was invented in northern Italy in the early 1400s as a card game. From those very mundane beginnings, Tarot has come to be used in a wide variety of ways by a wide variety of persons—for meditation; as inspiration for song, poetry, and film; for divination; for role-playing games; and, in some places, still, as a card game. My favorite way to use Tarot is as a tool for self-discovery.

Anything can be used for self-discovery: raindrops falling against a window, shadows falling on a wall, daydreams, animal messengers, spirit guides, synchronicity, fortune cookies, journaling, and more. Tarot is particularly useful for self-discovery because its seventy-eight cards portray many universal symbols and archetypes that work well with our subconscious minds.

I like to think of Tarot cards as a bridge connecting the conscious mind to the subconscious mind. Our subconscious minds have much to tell us, but they cannot speak directly to our conscious minds. Instead, they use dreams, hunches, and feelings. Tarot cards work very well to help us listen to and understand our subconscious. The subconscious mind does not communicate in complete sentences. Instead it uses pictures, images, fragments, representations, substitutions, and transferred references. Tarot cards can be extremely useful in helping us to decipher the messages from our subconscious since the pictures on the cards *speak* in the language of the subconscious—the language of symbols and pictures and imagination.

What Is Self-Discovery?

It is all very well and good to say that Tarot cards are excellent tools for self-discovery, but what exactly do I mean by self-discovery? Many people have a feeling that self-discovery is about warm, fuzzy feelings of self-love, self-acceptance, and healthy self-esteem. This is definitely one part of self-discovery. However, it is not the whole picture. Often, our conscious minds will suppress self-knowledge because it is painful or negative. For instance, I was talking to a friend, saying, "Remember when you got your hand caught in the car door?" Becky replied, "I sure do. You're the one who shut the door on my hand!" I had remembered that she had gotten hurt, but I had forgotten that I was the one who was the instrument of her pain. After she reminded me, I was able to play back the experience in my mind, and I realized that I had indeed shut a car door on my friend's hand, but that I had suppressed the part of the incident that was personally painful. After dealing with the pain and guilt that I felt, I was able to have a more accurate memory.

Often, we are unable to deal with a flaw or weakness in our personality, and we will either suppress or deny that knowledge. If we are to move on and grow, it is necessary to see our faults and flaws and to recognize them honestly. This can be extremely painful, extremely difficult, and many of us will need or want some help to deal with some of these issues—a friend, a counselor, or a therapist.

Some of us have a tendency to deny our flaws and faults and to attribute all of our failures to fate or to others. Others of us have a tendency to blame ourselves for everything—the failures not only in our own lives but in the lives of those around us. Some of us flipflop between both of these tendencies, sometimes falling to one side, sometimes to the other. Neither tendency is healthy; both are extremes to be avoided. The truth is in the middle.

For me, self-discovery is about discovering the truth in the middle and about learning to live life in balance. Sometimes self-discovery is painful, showing me my flaws, weaknesses, and mistakes. Sometimes self-discovery is full of joy and thanksgiving, showing me blessings and gifts and strengths that I had ignored or believed nonexistent.

Did I really throw sand in a boy's face when I was six? Yes, I did. Can I apologize to him? No, I do not remember his name or know where to find him. Do I feel guilty over this action from my childhood? Yes. There are countless incidents from my past that have often wracked me with guilt and pain and sorrow. Can I learn to accept this guilt, release it, and move on to areas of my life where I can make a positive difference? Yes. Indeed, not only can I, but I must, if I am to grow.

You can see that, to me, self-discovery is closely linked to growth. If I merely take self-knowledge and do nothing, then I run the danger of falling into negativity or egotism. I find that it is also important to balance the type of self-knowledge that I'm working on. If I'm tending toward depression and low self-esteem, then I work on ego-boosting self-knowledge. If I am feeling strong and positive about myself, then I'm in a good place to deal with some of my faults and flaws.

Some metaphysical teachers suggest to their students that they keep a journal where they write their positive qualities on one side of the journal and their negative qualities on the other side. The goal is to keep both sides in balance. Some of us tend to dwell on the positive, others on the negative. Both are necessary, for truth resides in the middle.

Self-knowledge is frequently contradictory. My journal frequently reveals this by expressing on one side, "I am lazy," and on another side, "I am hard-working." Both are true. Sometimes I am lazy, and sometimes I am hard-working. Like Emerson, I contradict myself gladly.

Self-discovery is difficult. It often takes great work, great effort. It takes time. It takes energy. It often takes brutal honesty, whether this is in acknowledging our talents or in admitting our faults, in giving validity to our hopes and dreams, and in giving voice to our unspoken fears.

Here again, balance is the keynote. Self-discovery must be balanced to keep our growth moving forward. Just as plants need both the coolness of night and the heat of day, the dryness of earth and the moisture of water, so do we need various elements and in healthy amounts. Sunlight is good, but too much sunlight leads to sunburn and heat stroke. Rain is good, but too much rain leads to flooding and root rot. Too much of a good thing becomes a bad thing in our own lives as well as in the life of a plant.

It is my belief that the Tarot is basically amoral, like most tools. That is, it can be used positively or used negatively, depending on the intent of the user. A hammer can be used to build a home, or a hammer can be used to inflict pain. The choice is not the hammer's but the user's. Tarot can be used to enlighten, or, unfortunately, in the hands of manipulative and power-obsessed persons, it can be used to frighten and control.

On its own, Tarot is neutral, except perhaps in one regard. There seems to be an inherent message of balance in the cards themselves. Over and over, the cards suggest that it is the middle way that we should seek, that extremes can be useful, but that living in an extreme state for a prolonged time is not healthy. Over and over, the cards show a central figure sitting or standing between two extremes: a white or black pillar, a man or a woman, a pair of sphinxes, twin towers, and more. Over and over, masculine is balanced with feminine, action is balanced with inaction, solar is balanced with lunar, light is balanced with dark, and Tarot makes no judgments against male or female, action or inaction, solar or lunar, or light or dark. The only judgment seems to be that both are needed, both are necessary, both are valuable.

Tarot teaches us not only this lesson about the duality of life; it also teaches us the lesson of balance with the four classical elements of air, fire, water, and earth. Water is not better than fire, nor earth than air. All four elements are necessary. All four have valuable lessons for us. All four have gifts and challenges for us.

Therefore, if a person were just to look at the deck of Tarot cards, over and over and over, I believe that he or she would learn valuable lessons about the nature of life and about how to live so that his or her life would be a vital life of growth and exploration. It is with this belief that I began to write exercises using the Tarot for self-discovery.

At this point I need to be very frank. I did not start writing Tarot for self-discovery exercises to help other people. I started writing them to help myself. I had reached a point in my Tarot studies where I was getting stale. I also had gotten out of touch with many of my old Tarot friends that I had known in a now-defunct computer network. I came up with Tarot for self-discovery as a way of resparking my own passion for Tarot and also reuniting me with my out-of-touch computer friends. I started an e-mail discussion group where I would post an exercise every week or so, and then the members of the list would work the exercises and comment on each other's work. At the outset, I did not intend to write original exercises, but rather to find exercises in various books and websites and to use the exercises of others. It was also my hope that members of the list would aid me in finding exercises to share. My plan succeeded admirably in one area and not at all in another area. It also surprised me in ways that I had no way of foreseeing.

Yes, my passion for Tarot was resparked. No, my friends did not flock to join the e-mail list. No, the way that the list was intended to work—as a community with each person commenting on the work of every other person and finding exercises for the group—did not work. However, this is not to say that the experiment was a failure. The experiment just went in directions that the designer had no way of predicting.

Was I disappointed? Yes. Was I pleased? Yes.

The Exercises

The first pleasant surprise was that I enjoyed writing original exercises and that I seemed to have a talent for it. People responded to the exercises that I wrote, and I abandoned the idea of looking for preexisting exercises to use with the group, since my own proved so popular. Most of the earliest exercises were prompted by events in my own life—weddings, sorrows, problems, and disappointments. Later, I began to take requests and to tailor exercises for others based on their needs. Surprisingly, music seems to have inspired many of the exercises. I did not realize how important music was in my life until I had written about twenty of the exercises. As you read through the exercises, you'll be reading, in part, a biography of my life for two years and also a library of the songs that I love.

Although the exercises vary, a few common elements run through most of them. First, Tarot for self-discovery exercises are about using Tarot for self-discovery and spiritual discovery. They are not really about learning Tarot, although you do learn Tarot if you work through these exercises. Tarot is our tool; self-discovery is our goal. As you work faithfully toward your goal, you get to know your tool very well. For many of the exercises, you can also use other kinds of cards and not just Tarot cards. However, they were designed to be used with Tarot and they seem to work best with Tarot.

Tarot for Self Discovery is not a substitute for therapy, either with a private therapist or group therapy. In some ways, however, doing these exercises can be as challenging and enlightening as some forms of therapy. If you work these exercises honestly, you will find that they reveal tough truths about yourself and about life. These exercises are sometimes easy, sometimes difficult, sometimes fun, sometimes thought-provoking, sometimes quick, and sometimes long—although they have much in common, there is much variety here too. The exercises are worthwhile for those who are brave and willing and who make the time to work them. Although I have written all of these exercises, they seem to have developed a life and energy of their own that goes beyond any intention or wisdom of mine.

These exercises will not fix problems in your life nor automatically change your life. Working one exercise will not solve your problems and enable you to live happily ever after. However, if you honestly work at a series of exercises and follow through by doing the concrete steps, you will find that your life will improve, that your self-understanding will be enriched, and that you will have blessed yourself in many ways that you had not even dreamed of.

Many of these exercises have a strong spiritual component as well. They are not a substitute for a personal spiritual practice, although they may certainly enhance your spiritual practice.

These exercises may be worked alone, or you may choose to work them with a friend or in a group. If you work them in a group, I do have a few suggestions. I would suggest making clear that working the exercises is not a form of group therapy. Your group should be committed to self-discovery and be prepared for surprises. A Tarot for self-discovery group is not a group for getting strokes or "Oh, you poor dear" comments. It is not a place for seeking sympathy (although you may find sympathy). It is not a place for seeking friendship (although you may find friendship). It is not a place for seeking free counseling (although you may benefit from free counsel that you receive). It is not a place to find a spiritual leader (although spiritual leadership will shine through from your fellow group members).

If you work these exercises honestly, you will find that they reveal tough truths. A group working these exercises will not be an easy group to participate in, but it will be worthwhile for those who are brave and willing, and who make the time to work the exercises. Be sure to stress that anything said at a group meeting stays in that meeting. Keep confidences within the group.

You can work the exercises in any order that you like. You can begin with any exercise and go from any exercise to any other exercise. I have broken the exercises into three groups: easy exercises, intermediate exercises, and exercises for special occasions or situations, but this division is just a general indication that you may feel free to ignore. Some of the exercises are light and funny. Other exercises are anything but light and funny. If you don't like one exercise, try another. There is a wide variety here, something for everyone. Pick and choose. Have fun.

If you really enjoyed an exercise, you can work it more than once. If you feel that you didn't quite "get it," you can also work an exercise again later. I don't recommend working more than a maximum of three exercises per week. Most people will find that one to two exercises per week work best. For others, one to two exercises per month will be best. Some people get so excited about the exercises that they want to do as many as they can, as fast as they can. Quality is more important than quantity. The exercises will be more powerful if you pace yourself. You will be discovering some deep truths, and you'll need time to assimilate these truths.

Take time and let the exercises soak in. Mull them over. Meditate on them. Ponder them. Let them go deep inside you. If you do too many too rapidly, it's sort of like coming up too quickly when you've been doing deep underwater diving—you'll get the bends.

While you're waiting, go back over the exercises that you've already worked and see if you get additional insights. Work on your concrete steps. Remember: Faster is not better.

As an aid in your Tarot for self-discovery work, I recommend keeping a journal of your exercise work. If you already have a Tarot journal, you may include these exercises in that journal. If you wish you may start a special journal just for these exercises. I recommend including the following information in your Tarot for self-discovery journal.

- Date

- Time of day

- Sign that the Sun is in

- Sign that the Moon is in

- Phase of the Moon

- Name of the exercise being worked

- Deck that you are using

- Any special factors to consider or events in your life that may impact on the working of these exercise

- Any grounding or centering or meditation that you do before beginning the exercise

- Your state of mind before starting the exercise

- Your exercise notes

- Your state of mind after the exercise

- Blank space for notes to be added later upon review

By reviewing your journal from time to time, you can gain additional insights into yourself. You may want to use a loose-leaf notebook for your journal, a blank book, or even a special file or folder on your computer. The important factor is that the format of your journal feel comfortable to you. Use whatever method you are most likely to stick with.

Working the Exercises

My students frequently comment, "I hope I did the exercise right!" Most of the time, "right" is not something that I focus on because there are lots of different "rights," and no one "right" is better than the next one.

I do have an overall suggestion for working the exercises. They seem to work best if you work them through as you read them. In other words, either don't read all of the way to the end, or, if you do, don't think about the end of the exercise. As you work the exercise, focus on the step that you are in, not on the next step or the final step.

In my experience, there are only two basic problems to watch out for in working the exercises. One is failing to narrow the card choices and trying to work an exercise with more cards than is feasible. The second is leaving off or misinterpreting what is, to me, the most important final step. Many times, without doing the final step or in misunderstanding the final step, the real effect of the exercise is missed.

The main reason to limit the choice to one card (or to however many cards are mentioned in the specific exercise) is to make the exercise manageable in length. Without limiting the number of cards used, an exercise can take six, seven, or eight hours. This is way too long to be practical. In addition, there are other reasons to limit the number of cards used in an exercise, primarily, in my opinion, because it is better to focus deeply on one card (or two or three cards) than to look more superficially on a great number of cards. After all, if you feel like you did not get all of the information you needed from an exercise, you can always go back and do it again later, this time using different cards. People are often surprised at how well this works, and often doing the exercise a second or third time can be even more powerful than the first time.

However, many people find themselves unable or unwilling to narrow the choices. What I suggest to people who have a hard time choosing is this. First, initially choose several cards. Then spread those cards before you and study them. Do you see themes? Can you see that you can group some of the cards together as being variations on a similar idea? If so, choose one card for each theme. Then, look at those chosen cards. Is there one that sums up the issue and your feelings more than the others? If so, choose it. If not, then work with the two or three representative cards that you have.

Also, if you just can't decide on one card, take all of your choices and turn them facedown. Mix them up, and then randomly choose a card. Work the exercise using this one card.

On the other hand, some of the exercises call for using several cards together, and some people have trouble with this. If you find yourself with this difficulty, here are some suggestions for using more than one card in an exercise.

Take some time to look at each card individually. See how it fits its position and you. It may not fit, or it may take some thought to make it fit. I have been known to turn to books myself when stumped, but when I wrestle with the cards by myself first, I usually do best. Even when I do resort to the books, the book insights are much richer for coming after my private wrestling over the cards.

After you've worked a bit with each card alone, you might break them into pairs and read two together or maybe three, if applicable. Look at how your cards are similar, how they are different. Which direction do the characters look? What is the mood or tone of each card? How are they alike? How different? What colors predominate? Are there any symbols that repeat each other? Are there any numerological relationships between the cards? Any thematic ones?

How does one card capture one side of you and another card capture another side of you? How well do those two sides of you work together? How well do the cards representing those sides work together? What aspects of yourself seem most evolved? Do the cards reflect this? If so, how? If not, how are they off?

Think of working with the cards as something like going flyfishing. You keep tossing out your lure until you get a bite, and then you play with it, reeling it in with as much finesse as you can master. Experience helps, but perseverance helps more than anything else, that and a willingness to play.

Other than failing to do the concrete step or using too many cards, I think that the exercises have a great deal of flexibility and can tolerate a lot of personal improvisation and mistake. Besides, who am I to say that by doing it *wrong*, you might not be doing it the right way for you? Might you not be getting more from the exercise by doing it wrong than by doing it right? That said, the exercises are carefully designed to be worked without leaving out steps, so please try to always finish the final step, which often is taking a concrete step of some kind.

Many people confuse a general plan or goal with a concrete step. A general plan or goal might be to study Tarot more, to learn more about a new spiritual practice, to meditate more, or to relax more. These are worthy goals, but they are not concrete plans. Concrete plans are generally something specific that you can do either immediately, in the next twenty-four hours, or, at the most, in a week. Let me clarify what a concrete step might be by giving examples.

- Letting someone else go in front of you in line

- Giving someone else your newspaper when you are done reading it

- Taking a load of cans and jars and papers to the recycling center

- Calling up an old friend

- Mailing an "I Love You" card to someone who lives in the same house

- Taking a walk

- Getting rid of three boxes of "stuff" that have been moving with you from home to home, but never getting used

- Meditating on a specific issue for twenty minutes, today (not planning on meditating later)

- Complimenting a harried or tired checkout clerk or telling her or him how much you appreciate her or his work

These are very specific actions. This is what I mean by concrete step in the exercises.

I cannot stress too much the importance of finishing the exercise, of going all of the way to the end and devising a concrete step and in carrying it out. Until you have completed your concrete step, you have not completed the exercise. By taking the concrete step, we begin to move beyond self-discovery into the realm of self-transformation.

It is one thing to become aware of ourselves, to discover deep inner secrets about ourselves and the world around us. However, knowledge alone is not enough. It is necessary to go beyond knowledge into action, which is why I normally include the concrete step.

So, we have a series of steps involved. First, we work the exercise in order to gain knowledge and understanding. Second, we devise a concrete step to take that will carry the knowledge into action in our lives and begin to work with our knowledge, making changes in our lives. Third, we must actually do the concrete step. Often, this is the hardest part. However, this is the most important part. If, in working through the exercise and the concrete step, you find that it isn't working, feel free to modify the concrete step into something that does work for you. The important thing is to do the transformational work, not to stick to your original plan.

In performing the concrete step, we find the true magic and mystery and power. This is where we remake ourselves. This is where we get things done. This is where our higher selves begin to manifest. This is where we begin to become all that we can be, where we begin to transform ourselves and to transform the world around us. All of the exercises in the world will not make any difference in us or our world unless we follow doing the exercises with action. All of the exercises in the world will be only moments of enlightenment unless we take that enlightenment and make changes in how we live.

In Tarot terms, we go from Swords (discovery) to Cups (feelings based on the discovery) to Wands (actions based on the discovery and feelings) to Pentacles (results based on actions).

A Note on Study

I am a firm believer in study. I believe in taking workshops, classes, and seminars. I believe in studying a wide variety of books. However, in these exercises, you'll see me over and over advise, "Don't look at the book. Go with your intuition. Go with your intuitive response."

In working these exercises, I do suggest that you temporarily put your books and studies aside. These exercises are primarily for teaching you about yourself, not Tarot. Therefore, what the experts have to say about a card is not as significant at the moment of working the exercise as your response is to the cards you are working with.

If you already have a wide knowledge of Tarot, you do not need to put it aside to work these exercises. Your knowledge will only enhance and reinforce the power of the exercises. You may find yourself needing sometimes to remind yourself to use your personal insights first and to supplement them with your body of knowledge, rather than the other way around.

These exercises work for beginners and more advanced students. The study of Tarot benefits us all, beginners and advanced students. However, the time for study is not in the middle of working an exercise for self-discovery. Study before doing an exercise or afterward, but, please, do not stop in the middle of an exercise to consult a book.

TWO

EASY TAROT FOR SELF-DISCOVERY EXERCISES

I call these exercises easy, and they are, compared to the other exercises. They also tend to be a bit more lighthearted than the intermediate exercises and the exercises for special occasions and situations. Anyone can do these exercises and anyone can do the other exercises as well. These just tend to be shorter than some of the others and require less background in Tarot and other related metaphysical disciplines. These exercises are a good place to start, to get your feet wet, so to speak, with the Tarot for Self-Discovery method. Don't feel that you have to do all of these before going on to the other exercises. Do them in any order that appeals to you and have fun with them.

Who Am I?

I was inspired on this exercise by the work of James Wanless, creator of the *Voyager Tarot*. This exercise is a basic Tarot teaching device, used by many teachers, but he is the person that I learned it from first.

Choose a Tarot deck. Enter the name and other pertinent information into your Tarot journal. Look through your deck faceup. Find the card that feels/looks/seems most like you. It should be the one card, more than any other card, you could show to a stranger and say, "This is me!" Choose the card that represents who you are at this moment. Yesterday you might have chosen differently. Tomorrow you might choose differently. Choose for now.

Describe this card. Then tell how you feel this card describes or shows who you are. What secrets about you does this card show? What about you does this card omit? What about this card is not like you? Do you think that others see you as this card? Why or why not? How is how they see you like/unlike how you see yourself?

Would you like to be more like this card or would you prefer to be more like another card? If you would like to be more like another card, what card? Why?

If you would like to make changes in who you are, either by becoming more like the first card you chose or becoming more like another card, think of at least one thing you can do this week that would help you move toward being more like the card you aspire to. What is that action? Make a commitment to taking that action as soon as possible.

Tell Me a Story

Choose a Tarot deck. Record it and other information in your Tarot journal. Go through your deck faceup and choose a card with a prominent main character, someone who could be the leading character in a story you'd like to tell. Pull that card out and lay it in front of you. Next, shuffle your deck, and deal four cards off the top. Lay them out in order: one, two, three, four.

Tell us a story based on your five cards. If you have trouble coming up with an ending, you have permission to go through the deck faceup in order to find one card which would bring the story to a close that suits you.

Any interesting insights? Any striking parallels to your own life? Any striking discrepancies to your own life? Would you like your life to be more like your story or less? Why?

If you made a movie of your story, who would you cast in the leading role? Why?

Picture This

This is a short and sweet exercise, but it has proven extremely powerful for many who have worked it. Do not read ahead on this exercise. Do it as you read.

Choose your Tarot deck. Record it in your Tarot journal. Separate the Major Arcana from the Minor Arcana. Go through the Major Arcana, faceup. Choose a card that seems least friendly to you, possibly even horrible or frightening. Study the card carefully. Find a picture of someone you don't like, even if it is from the newspaper or television screen. You can choose someone that you don't like or someone that you find truly abhorrent. Look at the picture of the person that you have chosen. Mentally paste this person's face on to one of the faces of the card, preferably the face of the main character. (Some of you who are so inspired might want to do this physically as well as mentally, especially if you have a scanner and a good graphics program on your computer or access to a photocopier so that you don't have to injure your actual Tarot card.)

Look at the card again—the modified version, and describe your feelings and reactions at seeing this person's face looking out at you from your chosen Tarot card. Do you feel differently about the card with your disliked person's face on it? How so? Is the card more horrific to you or more real? Are your reactions different? If so, how?

Now, find a picture of a baby. If you have a picture of yourself as a baby, this is preferred. A picture of one of your children or grandchildren or any other person that you have loved is also good. If you don't have a baby picture of yourself or a loved one, a picture of a baby from a magazine will do. Look at the face of the baby. Mentally paste the baby's face onto the face in this Major Arcana card. (Again, you may physically paste this picture onto a copy or a scan of the card if you wish.)

Look at the card again, seeing the baby's face on the card. Describe your feelings and reactions. Do you feel differently about the card with the baby's face on it? How so? Is the card more positive to you or more horrific? Are your reactions different? If so, how?

Look in the mirror. See your face clearly. Now, mentally, paste your face onto a face in this Major Arcana card. (Again, you may physically paste this picture onto a copy or a scan of the card if you wish.)

Look at the card again, this time seeing your face in the card. Describe your feelings and reactions. Do you feel differently about the card with your face on it? How so? Is the card more positive to you or more horrific? Are your reactions different? If so, how?

How was it different to see someone that you didn't like in this card than seeing a baby or seeing yourself? Record in your journal any insights that you may have into the Tarot or yourself. No concrete step for this exercise.

As a variation on this exercise, you can do it in reverse. You can take a card that you really like, one that feels very positive for you. You can put the same three pictures on the card, in the same order, and go through the same steps. It is very illuminating to see how our reactions change with using these same three pictures on a positive card from our reactions to using them with a negative card.

Whose Life Is It Anyway?

I contend that there is no one absolutely right and true way to read Tarot cards. The same three cards will mean different things to different people. This is because the cards, although based on universal symbols, truths, and archetypes, also work with our individual subconscious minds. Each mind is different. Each life is different.

In reading Tarot as a form of self-discovery, there is some importance in which cards actually come up, but there is more importance in how you react to the cards. There are messages that your subconscious is trying to get to your conscious, and the Tarot is an excellent form of communicating these messages from one part of the brain to another.

That said, draw three cards at random from your deck. Don't look at them yet. Place them aside for now. You are going to do a series of short readings with the same three cards. In doing these readings, since this is primarily an exercise for self-discovery, go with your own instincts first; later, if you feel you must, you can look up the cards in a book. If you look at a book first, you may choke or stifle your intuition. If you go with your intuition first, you can always still look at a book later.

Use your favorite deck and your favorite three-card spread. Some popular choices are Body-Mind-Spirit, Thesis-Antithesis-Synthesis, and Person A's View-Person B's View-the Middle Way. There are a great many good three-card spreads that will work for this exercise although I don't recommend the Past-Present-Future spread. Record your deck and choice of spread in your Tarot journal. You are going to do three separate readings with the same three cards, using the same deck.

For the first two readings, you're going to be reading for someone else. First, you will read for a celebrity. You need to use someone whose life is familiar to you. Don't chose a celebrity if you don't know much about that person's life. It can be someone you admire or someone you dislike. It can be a historical figure like Hitler or Joan of Arc or it can be someone from popular culture like Whoopi Goldberg, Robin Williams, Oprah Winfrey, Madonna, Tina Turner, Eric Clapton, or a member of your favorite rock band or singing group. You can choose an athlete or a politician. Choose the person before you begin the reading; do not begin the reading until you have the person firmly in mind.

Do your reading for your celebrity. Record it in your journal.

Second, you are going to read for a friend or a family member. You will use the same three cards from the same deck, but you may use either a different spread or the same spread. Record this reading in your journal.

Finally, when you have finished these two readings, do a third reading with these same cards, but this time the reading is for you. This will be a different reading, not just substituting yourself in the place of the other person. Read freshly each time, applying the cards to what you know of each person's life.

How are the three readings different? How are they the same? Have you read the cards in the same way for yourself as for the other persons? How were the readings different for you, your friend or family member, and the celebrity? What does this tell you about how the cards can vary in meaning and interpretation and yet also have a core or essence of similarity? What does this say to you about the meanings of the cards and about how they work with your subconscious? Which reading do you like best? Why?

In this exercise, we learn something new about the Tarot and about individual cards, more so than in most of the other exercises. Never fear, you should learn something about yourself through this exercise as well. No concrete step.

Happy Feet

Those of you who are baby boomers will easily remember Steve Martin's early stand-up routine. He would play his banjo, put an arrow through his ears (well, not really), and do his "happy feet" dance. Basically, according to Martin's routine, when you have "happy feet," anything can happen. Those happy feet just keep going, and they can take you into unusual places, just dancing away with you. The concept is sort of like a positive spin on the story of the red shoes.

One thing that I have discovered is that if one part of you is very very happy, the happiness is contagious. So, if our feet are happy, pretty soon the rest of us is happy too. If our tongues are happy eating something fun and fizzy that tickles our tongues, the rest of us gets happy. We are going to use the concept of contagious happiness in this exercise.

Choose a Tarot deck. Record it in your Tarot journal. Go through your deck, faceup, and look for happy feet. Choose the card which, to you, has the happiest feet. Describe the card and tell why you think it has happy feet. Have your feet ever felt that happy? Tell how so or why not.

Now, think of a sad, glum day. Go through your deck and choose a card that most closely resembles how you felt on that sad, glum day. What is the card? How does it fit your sad, glum day?

Now, in your mind's eye, take the happy feet of your first card, and apply them to the legs of a character in your second card. What happens in the second card when the happy feet take over? Describe a scene or action that might take place if the person in the sad, glum card had happy feet.

What might happen in your own life if you let happy feet take over? What can you do today with happy feet? Devise a concrete step for something to do today with happy feet. Remember to be specific.

Gotta Dance

Think about what dance means to you personally. There will be some elements common to all of us for dance, but there is a great variety as well. For some of us, dance is a social event. For others, dance is an art form. For some, dance is an expression of spiritual truth. Some people dance slowly, regally. Others dance in a wild frenzy. Some of us have a variety of dance styles, depending on our mood and the occasion. Pick your favorite expression of dance and record it in your Tarot journal.

Record your choice of Tarot deck in your journal. Go through your deck faceup. Find a card that best pictures what dance means to you. What is the card? How does it depict dance to you? Does it make you want to dance yourself? What feelings about dance does it bring up for you? Please discuss any and all impressions or feelings about this card as they relate to dance. Be thorough.

Now put your card back in your deck. Shuffle your deck. Choose a card, facedown. (You may cut and pick the top card, choose a card on a cut, or choose a card from a fanned-out, facedown deck, or however else you wish. Just choose a facedown card, one that you can't see its face.)

Turn your card over. What is it? What does this card tell you about dance? This may be easy, or it may be difficult, but find some way to relate this second card to dance. For instance, how would this card dance? What kind of dance would it be? Would you like to dance like this card? Does how this card would dance remind you of anyone or anything? What kind of music would this card dance to?

Finally, compare the two cards as they relate to dance. Which do you prefer and why? As a concrete step, devise a dance that incorporates elements of both cards and dance the dance. How do you feel?

Does it feel alien to you to incorporate the other elements into your dance? Does it feel like an adventurous stretch to incorporate those elements? Record your feelings in your journal.

Love Break

Lots of times we get busy with life, rushing and rushing and rushing, and we get caught up in the business of life. We get swept away by tension and anxiety and fear. What we need is a little love break—a short, quick, effective way to get in touch with sensations of love. I hope that this exercise will provide that way.

Go through your deck faceup, slowly, looking carefully at the pictures. Every time you find a card that sparks a little tug from your heart, set it aside. When you get done, look again through the cards you have set aside.

This time, think back to experiences of love. Everyone has some love in his or her life, although, unfortunately, some people do not have a lot. The more you feel love, the more you attract love, and this exercise is to help us to feel love more often throughout the day. So, remember love and feel love in order to attract more love into your life. Love may be your grandmother's lap. Love may be a childhood pet. Love may be romance. Love may be holding a child. Love may be a childhood playmate. Love may be a warm smile from a stranger. Love may be a pat on the back and a quick hug. Love can be all of these to us and more.

While looking slowly through the cards that you have set aside, pick two to four of them that most make feelings of love well up inside you. They may remind you of special persons in your life. They may remind you of special situations. It doesn't matter, but find two to four cards which, when you allow yourself to emotionally relate to the images on the cards, spark feelings of love.

Record these cards in your Tarot journal. These are to be the cards for your love breaks. For a few days or a week, try to keep these cards handy, either mentally or physically. When you find yourself feeling worried or depressed or lonely or anxious, pull out one of those cards (mentally or physically) for a love break. Look at the card closely (or reconstruct it mentally). See the card, either by focusing on it deliberately or by mentally focusing on it. Put your hand over your heart if you can. Allow yourself to relax into the love that the card represents for you. Allow yourself to feel the love that the card symbolizes for you.

"Fall" into the card. Enter into the realm of love that the card represents for you. If you have trouble falling into the card, just focus on it. The idea is not to make up a story about the card, or to try and get a reading from the card, or to think on the meaning of the card, but to focus on the emotion that the card calls up within you, to allow yourself to feel the love that the card represents for you.

To clarify, almost everyone will have a welling up of emotion at the picture of a baby, a kitten, or a puppy. An instinctive sort of "Awwww" comes forth. Sometimes beautiful landscapes will do the same, or pictures of someone giving a hug or a close-up of a flower. I took this known phenomenon and applied it to Tarot. You pick a card (or cards) that prompts that "Awwww" within you, and then you focus on that card (or one of your choices) during the day in order to deliberately initiate the welling up of love from within. In other words, you are planning on bringing love into your life with little mini-breaks. Repeat as often as you like, two or more times per day, rotating the cards. In this way, several times a day, you know that you are going to feel love.

How does this change your life—having built-in love breaks? After you've worked with this technique for a while, record the results in your Tarot journal. Tell about one or more of your love break experiences. How did you feel? What effect in your life did taking a love break have? What overall changes have you seen from the regular practice of taking love breaks?

Variation: Love Break for Two

This variation is based on the work of one of the members of my e-mail group. It is a good way to introduce Tarot to someone who is unfamiliar or uncomfortable with Tarot. It is also an excellent way to find out about differences in love expectations and relationships needs.

With the partner of your choice, using either different decks or taking turns with the same deck, go through the deck faceup, slowly, looking carefully at the pictures. Set aside the cards that tug at your heart with a wellspring of love. When each of you gets done, look through the cards you have set aside. (If you are sharing a deck, make a list of the cards that each chooses.)

Narrow each pile down to four or five cards. How are the cards that you chose different from the cards that your partner chose? What does this say about each of you and your approaches to love? Your expectations of love? How is this knowledge helpful to you as you think about your relationship?

Stages of Life

Shuffle your deck. Cut in whatever fashion you prefer. By your preferred method, choose three cards without looking at the faces. Turn the cards over. All cards will be read upright. Record the cards and the name of your deck in your Tarot journal.

It can be said that each of us contains the entire Tarot within us. Therefore, no matter what card you get, you can apply it to yourself. Take each of your three cards and find a way to apply it to your childhood or adolescence. You may use any symbol, any part of the card. You don't necessarily need to use traditional or conventional interpretations. In fact, you may do better if you go with your instant or gut impulse.

Then take each card and find a way to apply it to your present situation. You may want to be very literal. You may want to be very symbolic or allegorical.

Finally, take each card and find a way to apply it to a possible future direction that your life might take. This should be something that could happen; you can stretch things a bit, but try to keep it within the realm of possibility, even if a distant possibility. How possible or probable is this possibility? Do you want this possibility to happen? What can you do to make it happen? If you don't want it to happen, what can you do to ensure that it doesn't happen?

Devise a concrete step to take to work with your preference for the possible future indicated by these cards.

I Started a Joke

Jokes can be wonderful ways to defuse tension, to help us to relax, and to find humor in a stressful situation. Some jokes, however, are unkind, and I don't advocate the use of cruel humor. I am terrible at telling jokes, but, when I'm in front of a crowd, I am very funny. Jokes and a sense of humor and being funny are all different expressions of a similar energy. Jokes, as something that can be learned and told and retold by different people, can be enlightening when we examine them, revealing much that was at first hidden, both about the origina-tor of the joke and of all of those who repeat it.

I frequently turn to the Tarot for solace, but I rarely turn to the Tarot when I need a good laugh. This exercise uses Tarot as a source for laughter and fun.

As Tarot cards go, in most decks, I tend to favor both the Fool and the Magician for jokesters. To me, the Fool is more of a physical humor, more of a broad humor, more of the "big belly laugh and fall on the floor" sort of humor. The Fool does pratfalls and takes pies in the face. He may be a bit gross in his humor. The Magician has more of the quick wit, the verbal humor, the "raise your eyebrow and chuckle" sort of humor. He may be snide. He may stab you in the back with his remarks, but he does so with such charm and a smile that it isn't until later that you realize that you've been laughing while you've been insulted.

However, any Tarot card can be interpreted humorously. Several of the newer decks are wonderfully funny, with a great sense of play. Choose a Tarot deck. If you have a deck that seems to you to be a fun deck, use that one. Go through your deck, faceup, and choose a card to be your jokester. You can choose the Fool, the Magician, or any other card that you like. The card just needs to say to you, "I have a sense of humor. I want to make you laugh." This choice may be unique to the deck that you are using. Some cards are very funny in some decks and totally serious in others. No one else may find your choice funny. You, at this moment, using whatever deck you choose, need to find a card that, to you, says, "I'm a comedian."

What deck are you using? What card did you choose? Why do you think that it is funny?

Take the rest of your deck and shuffle. Using whatever method you prefer, choose five cards without looking at them. Lay them out in a row, left to right. Turn them over. What are they? These cards are the basis of your joke.

Jokes have many forms. Jokes can be puns. Jokes can be short. Jokes can be long and convoluted stories. Jokes can be "inside jokes" that only a few understand. It doesn't matter. Using the five cards for inspiration, have your comedian tell a joke. You can let the joke have five parts, each part closely tied to an individual card, or you can just take loose inspiration from your five cards.

By loose inspiration, I mean that the cards are related to the joke but not specifically. For instance, if you have the Tower, the Queen of Cups, the Knight of Cups, the 6 of Swords, and the High Priestess, you could come up with a joke about a camel (Hebrew letter assigned to the High Priestess in some systems) and a shipwreck (Tower combined with the Cups cards and the 6 of Swords, all of which show water).

Tell us your joke, long or short, complex or simple. Remember to tell it through the persona of your comedian, not your own voice. (This may be hard for some of you.) This can be a real joke, or it can just be a funny or amusing story.

What is it about this joke that appeals to you? Now, go through your deck, faceup, and choose the card that to you is the least funny card in the deck. What is it? Why is this card not funny? Imagine your joke if the character in this card tried to tell it. Would it be funny? Why or why not?

What does this say to you about your sense of humor? Is your joke or story funnier as told by your chosen comedian or is it funnier when it comes from an unexpected source? Some of the funniest moments in my life have been when someone unexpected says something. For example, in most decks, one of the least funny cards is the 10 of

Swords. However, I can imagine a hilarious *Monty Python* sort of skit narrated by the person in the 10 of Swords. How does the joke change when you change the joke-teller? Can you imagine how funny it is when this normally very unfunny card is in a funny situation?

Now find some way that this story mirrors your life. Which version of the joke more closely mirrors your life, the first version with the funny narrator or the second version? Why? How?

What secret or surprise about you does this joke reveal? Are you familiar with the term "Freudian slip"? Often, when we *accidentally* use one word in place of another, we are revealing our hidden thoughts or motives. In the first draft of this exercise, I accidentally typed the word "money" instead of the word "moment." In doing so, I revealed my financial worries to anyone who was a careful and perceptive reader.

Similarly, when we make a joke, we may do the same. If a wife makes a joke about her husband forgetting their anniversary, is she only being funny? Or is she also revealing her inner hurt? If a teenager makes a joke about being picked last in gym class for a team, is he just being funny, or is he also revealing his inner hurt?

Do you have an inner hurt that your joke reveals? How can you use humor to heal your hurt, not just reveal it? Come up with at least one positive way to use humor in your life within the next twenty-four hours. What is this concrete step? Record it in your Tarot journal and resolve to complete it.

My Tarot Neighborhood

Anyone ever play any of those Sim games? SimCity, SimEarth, Sim-Farm, SimAnts, The Sims? The newest one (at the time of this writing), The Sims, is all about constructing your own neighborhood and neighbors. In this exercise, you are going to construct your own neighborhood, out of Tarot cards.

First, decide what you want (what you really, really want) in a neighborhood. What's important to you in a neighborhood? For me, I would have to be near a bookstore or library. I would also need lots of trees nearby and a grassy area. I wouldn't have to have my own yard, but I'd need to be able to look out of the window and see grass and trees.

What do you really want in a neighborhood? Write it all down in your Tarot journal. How many neighbors do you want to have—lots or just a few? Write down the details. What kinds of neighbors do you want? Get it all on paper (or on your computer if you are more comfortable with a keyboard than with paper and pen). Look over your list and decide what parts you want and what parts you really, really want in your neighborhood. Highlight the most important elements for you.

Choose a Tarot deck or decks. Record the name of your deck or decks. Go through your Tarot deck(s), faceup. Populate your neighborhood with Tarot cards. You may feel free to use some cards more than once. Give reasons for making your choices.

Now, put your Tarot neighbors around you, either at your table or desk or on the floor. Put yourself in the center of your neighborhood. Look around your neighborhood; look at all your neighbors. How do you feel? Do you feel at ease, comfortable? Do you feel uncomfortable? Are there too many people around? Not enough people? Do you need more green? Do you need more water? Revise your Tarot neighborhood until you feel right in the center of it. Do you want to be at the center? Would you prefer to be on the edge, along the outskirts? Keep working and changing until the neighborhood feels right to you.

If you could change any one thing in your current neighborhood to make it more like your Tarot neighborhood, what would it be? Why? Is this a feasible change to make? If not, is there anything you actually could change to make your neighborhood more like your Tarot neighborhood? What is it? Remember the ripple effect. Sometimes big changes begin as a chain reaction from little changes.

Devise a concrete step for beginning one area of change for you in your current neighborhood. Resolve to begin making your first change now, big or small. The important thing is not the size of your change, but that you do it and not just contemplate doing it.

Synchronicity

Synchronicity is a term popularized by the psychologist Carl Jung. For the purpose of this exercise, I am going to use the phrase "meaningful coincidence" as a working definition of synchronicity.

All of us experience coincidence on a frequent basis. Some would go so far as to say that there is no such thing as coincidence, that all things that seem to be a coincidence are not coincidental at all. I would not go so far as that, but I would say that some coincidences seem to be more meaningful than others. The "catch" is that sometimes we can feel that a coincidence is meaningful in some way but we aren't sure exactly what the meaning is. This exercise is designed to find meaning in coincidences that feel meaningful but whose meaning is not clear.

Have in mind a particular series of events, ideas, concepts, or happenings that seem coincidental and that have an unclear meaning. Record a brief statement about these coincidences in your Tarot journal. Choose a Tarot deck, go through it, faceup, and find one card that seems to represent the unifying concept, theme, or event of the coincidences. What is the name of the card? How does it signify the coincidences to you?

Look at the card carefully. Study it. Write a paragraph on what draws you visually about the card. At this point, do not interpret the card; merely look, observe, and comment. You may add comments about how it seems to represent the coincidences, but do not try to get further meaning at this time and do not try to make a prediction or suggest a future action at this time.

Now, either shuffle your deck, or turn it over and swoosh all of the cards together or choose yet another way to mix your cards up without looking at them. By the method of your choice, choose, facedown, one card for each coincidental episode or incident. You may have from two to five cards, one for each one of the coincidences. Keeping the cards facedown, arrange them in a shape or pattern around the first card that you chose. You may arrange them in a line, or you may put the first card in the center of a triangle, or you may put a rainbow of cards over the first card, or anything else that comes to you. The shape will vary somewhat, depending on how many cards you are using. The central card or focus card should be, however, the first card that you chose. Find an arrangement that seems satisfactory to you, and then turn the additional cards over.

Study the layout as a whole. Look for common thematic material. Do not try to interpret the cards individually. The goal is to use the randomly chosen cards to find the meaning behind the synchronicity. We want to find a uniting meaning, not a series of individual meanings. What is the meaning?

Based on the message from the cards about the meaning of the synchronicity, decide on a concrete action to take. What is that action?

To illustrate, in my life, two friends and I all had dreams of a person who at one time in our lives had been extremely active and important. None of us had seen that person for over a year, maybe even two years; yet, during the same week, she was on all of our minds. This seemed to us to be a meaningful coincidence, but I wasn't quite clear on the meaning.

For the person that we all had on our minds, using the *Giant Rider-Waite* deck, I chose the Strength card, reversed. The person was an outgoing and generous person, but there were ego issues at times. When I looked at the card, I kept focusing on the mountains in the background of the card. To represent our three dreams, I randomly chose two Aces and the Lovers. I arranged them in a rainbow over the Strength card, reversed. What struck me in looking at these cards together is that all of the commentary cards had clouds, indicating that there has been a time of confusion, a time of hiding. All three of these cards showed someone or something coming out from behind the cards, indicating that now, perhaps, there was a time for change.

All four cards, the original card and the later three cards, have mountains in the background. Often, in Tarot, mountains indicate enlightenment, where we go for healing and renewal. I decided that the meaning of the synchronicity was that it was time for us all to heal from the rift with the other person. All of us had gone on with our lives, but there was some healing still remaining, and perhaps healing together was the best way to do this rather than to continue to work on healing alone.

For my concrete step, I decided to call my friends and arrange for us to perform a healing ritual together.

THREE

INTERMEDIATE TAROT
FOR SELF-DISCOVERY
EXERCISES

These exercises are more challenging than the ones in chapter 2. They tend to be longer, to have more complex steps, and require more background in Tarot and other related metaphysical disciplines. That said, many people with very little background or experience find that they can do these exercises and benefit from them. These exercises, as a whole, are less light-hearted than the easy ones and tend to encourage each person to delve more deeply into forgotten realms. They also hold more potential for growth, change, and transformation.

I'm the Top

I like to listen to popular music from the 30s and 40s. These songs were hits before I was born, but many of them have great appeal to me. One of my favorites is "You're the Top" by Cole Porter. In this song, the singer compares his/her love interest to such "tops" as the feet of Fred Astaire, an O'Neill drama, *Whistler's Mother*, Camembert, a rose, Dante, the nose of Jimmy Durante, a Berlin ballad, an old Dutch master, a Waldorf salad, a baby grand, a hot tamale, a Botticelli, Keats, Shelley, Ovaltine, the Tower of Babel, Mahatma Gandhi, a Shakespeare sonnet, Mickey Mouse, and so on. As originally performed on Broadway by Ethel Merman and William Gaxton, this song was extremely popular, even with seven verses and two refrains. In such a long song, the love interest gets compared to a lot of "tops."

As you can tell, the lover used not only a large number but also a wide variety of metaphors to get the point across. The main point was that the love object really and most sincerely is *the top*. The love object isn't just the top in one way. The love object is the top in all ways.

As much as I really enjoy this song, I think it's time for a little revision. Most of us have little trouble coming up with a long list of how our love objects are the top, but what about ourselves? How easy/hard is it to come up with a list of our own top qualities? Many of us have trouble when the tables are turned and we have to come up with ways that we are the top.

Perhaps the worst time of all is just after we've finished a major project or made a real accomplishment. Instead of relaxing, looking back, and thinking, "Wow! I just accomplished something great!" we often think, "So what? If I were really something, I would have done _____ instead."

Whether you are in that frame of mind, or just not appreciating yourself on other grounds, I invite you to do the "I'm the Top" exercise. This exercise, if done sincerely and completely, is designed to help improve your self image.

Choose your Tarot deck and record it in your Tarot journal. Go through your deck, faceup, looking for what you consider the best cards in the deck. You can choose from the Major or Minor Arcana or both. Narrow your selections down to five to ten cards. Which cards do you think are the five to ten best cards in your deck?

Name at least one way that you are like the positive qualities of each card. In other words, if you have chosen the Star, you will name at least one way that you are like the positive qualities of the Star. You must praise yourself wholly and completely. You are not permitted to say, "Well, on my good days, sometimes I am capable of being a little bit like this card in that I _____." Neither are you permitted to list ways in which you might be like the negative qualities of your good cards. This is a good-things-only exercise. Save the negative stuff for another day.

I suggest that you phrase your findings like affirmations and list them in your journal like this:

> *Like the Star, I reach out to others with hope and encourage-*
> *ment. Like the Hermit, I shine a light of wisdom and com-*
> *passion for others to see. Like the Fool, I step bravely into the*
> *unknown of new possibilities.*

You may choose more than one quality for each card, but you must choose at least one for each card. After you have recorded the ways that you are like the positive qualities of your cards, put them before you. Look at them carefully. Then, one by one, pick up your cards, gaze intently at each one, and say your statement or affirmation. Then say, "I am _____ (insert name of the card)."

In other words, while gazing intently at the Star, I might say, "I reach out to others with hope and encouragement. I am the Star." How did this feel? Was it hard to do?

Did you find that some cards were easier for you than others? If so, which ones? Do you have any ideas about why? If so, record your ideas in your journal.

Next, come up with a concrete step for each card that will rein-force your wonderful qualities. For instance, with our Star example, I might decide that going to visit someone in a nursing home would be a way to "reach out to others with hope and encouragement." I make a commitment to visit a specific person on a specific day, at a specific time (tomorrow, 2 P.M. in the afternoon, visit Geneva at the nursing home).

You should end up with five to ten concrete steps (depending on how many cards you chose) that will serve to reinforce qualities you already have within you. Don't feel like you have to do all of these steps right away. Space them out so that you don't feel overwhelmed. Do put them on your calendars, though, and do make a serious com-mitment to accomplish each of your concrete steps. After you've done each one of your concrete steps, go back to your entry for this exercise in your journal. Record your feelings about the experience. Do you feel any differently about yourself and/or the card after doing your concrete step? If so, how?

Finally, I challenge you to look over your statements and your cards each day for a week. See if you feel any better about yourself. See if there are any changes in your life, internal or external. Record your observations about this experience in your journal as well.

Jump-Start

Ever been kind of stuck in a rut or low on energy? You have exciting new goals, new projects, new dreams—but, somehow, you're having trouble finding the energy to get started with these plans. If you can ever get yourself going, you do fine. It's just finding that initial boost of energy that's the problem, getting the motivation to get up and make those changes.

This exercise is to help get you jump started, to gain and use that initial boost of energy. It is related to (but different from) the "Miracle" exercise and the "Bone Weary/Soul Weary" exercise. It also has some similarities to the "Maybe Later" exercise. This particular exercise was written at the request of a member of my e-mail group.

In your life, you may have several areas where you need to get jump started, or you may have just one. For the purpose of this exercise, please choose one area. Later, you can repeat the exercise for other areas if you wish. Record the area of life that you are going to work on in this exercise in your Tarot journal. Choose a Tarot deck and enter it in your journal as well.

Think of an area of life where you lack motivation, where you're having trouble getting your energy going. What area of life is this? (You can be general or specific.) Now, think of three wonderful reasons not to go ahead in this area of your life, three wonderful reasons not to get started, and three wonderful reasons to just sit there and let this opportunity slide by. Write these three reasons down.

Go through your Tarot deck, faceup, and choose a card to represent the area of your life where you need motivation, and then also choose a card for each reason to delay. Record in your journal what the cards are and how they fit your area of no motivation and your reasons for not acting. What do you learn from looking at these cards and studying them?

Now, take your remaining cards and shuffle them. Facedown, choose three cards to serve as reasons to get started. Put each card over one of the three cards representing reasons not to get started. In other words, *assign* one of these newer cards (chosen without looking) to each of the three previously chosen cards for a reason not to go ahead. Either put the new cards next to the first cards or directly over them. At this time, the first card that you chose, the one representing your area needing to be jump-started, is still alone, uncovered and unpaired with any other card.

What are these newer cards? Think about using the energy of each of these cards to help you deal with your reasons not to go ahead. How could each one be seen as an answer or cure or antidote to your reason not to go ahead? Record your insights.

Now, you are going to do some chaos magic. Take your cards and shuffle them or shake them or riffle them vigorously. As you do so, concentrate on what you need as a "kick in the posterior." Keep vigorously shaking or shuffling or riffling until a card falls out. This is your jump-start card, the one that will give you the much-needed kick in the posterior. What is it? How can this card represent a kick to get you jump started?

Put your jump-start card first with each of your three pairs of cards. Read the jump-start card with each pair. How is reading these three sets of three cards different from reading only the two cards together? What insights does your jump-start card bring to each of the three pairs? Think of a concrete action for each of these three groupings. Record the concrete step to take in your journal.

Finally, take your jump-start card and pair it with the first card you chose, the one that described the area of your life needing the jump-start. Study this pair of cards. What does the jump-start card tell you about the area of your life needing to be jump started? Sometimes it tells us that the reason that we are delaying is a good one. Be open to all interpretations, even surprising ones.

To clarify, if your three cards representing reasons today were the Ace of Pentacles, the Chariot, and the Page of Cups, and your second three cards happened to be the Moon, the Page of Wands, and the 3 of Wands, and if your jump-start card was the Tower, you would read first the Ace of Pentacles with the Moon, the Chariot with the Page of Wands, and the Page of Cups with the 3 of Wands. Then you would read your jump-start card (in this case, the Tower) with each of those pairs.

After recording all of your insights, you are to come up with one concrete action to resolve the problem of each of your reasons to not act. You will end up with three concrete steps or actions at the end of this exercise, all united by the energy of the jump-start card. As a final insight, you'll look at your jump-start card with your first-chosen card, the one that represents your area of life needing to be jump-started.

Sliding

This exercise is one of my personal favorites and also a favorite of my students and e-mail group members. It originated out of some discussion on another exercise. Inspiration, as always, comes from a variety of places.

You can choose to do this exercise in a playful manner or in a more serious manner, depending on your own mood. I'd like to encourage people to try it playfully, thinking of being a child and physically sliding from one place to another. I think of it like a kitten sliding up and down on piano keys. If you are a fan of the television program *Sliders*, you may want to think of yourself as a character on that program.

Choose your deck and record it in your Tarot journal. Separate your deck into Majors and Minors. (For those new to Tarot, there are twenty-two Majors, cards like Strength, the Magician, the Star, the Chariot. There are fifty-six Minors, and they are usually called "Something" of Swords, Wands, Cups, and Pentacles or some variation of these names.)

Put your Major Arcana aside. You will not use it for this particular exercise. Look at your Minor Arcana faceup. You will see some cards that make you smile, and others that make you a bit anxious. Choose one of the cards that makes you uncomfortable, which makes you a bit anxious. (Don't choose anything that alarms you unduly, just something that feels slightly uncomfortable.) What is it? Record it in your journal, along with what it is about the card that makes you uncomfortable. Describe your feelings and reactions. You may also describe what you see on the card. Do not interpret the meaning of the card, only your reactions to it and what you see on the card itself.

Now, go through your deck and choose the other three cards of the same rank as your first card. In other words, if you chose the 5 of Pentacles, go through and choose the other 5s. If you chose the 10 of Swords, go through and choose the other 10s. Depending on the deck that you are using and the card that you originally started with, it may be that none of the four cards makes you very comfortable.

Line up all four cards, from least comfortable to most comfortable. What order did you put the cards in? Why? Do you see a progression of any kind? What insights do you get about yourself when you look at your four cards, ranged from least comfortable to most comfortable?

Think of each card as being a separate world or universe or place. Perhaps you might think of each of them as a storefront at a mall or festival. What would it take to *slide* from the least-comfortable card to the next one? What would it take for you to move from one world to the next? From one place to another, as represented by your cards? Can you do it?

It helps some people to think of the concept of sliding in reference to musical scales. Think of sliding from a major chord to a minor chord. The difference is subtle, but the effect is noticeable. The mood is different in a major chord and in a minor chord. The chords might be in the same key, but they are not the same. Similarly, a 10 of Pentacles and a 10 of Cups are both 10s, but they are not the same. They are related, but they are different. By concentrating on their similarities, we can mentally move or shift from the concept of one to the concept of the other.

Think of the seasons. We don't go from winter directly to summer; we go from winter to spring to summer to autumn and back to winter. We ease into the change, slowly, naturally, almost effortlessly. This is what sliding is about. It is gradual transformation in stages and steps that doesn't shock our systems.

In Tarot, what would it take to slide from the world or situation of the 6 of Pentacles to the world or situation of the 6 of Cups? They are very similar, but one may feel more comfortable to you than the other. Why? What is the difference? If you are in the world of the 6 of Pentacles, can you change your situation or your attitudes to make things more like the 6 of Cups? How?

For example, if you are feeling like one of the persons whose hands are reaching up for coins in the 6 of Pentacles, how could you change your attitudes and feelings to be more like the little girl in the 6 of Cups? (I'm referring to the *Rider-Waite-Smith* pictures here. Your images will change, depending on the deck you are using.) Take that sliding step, at least in your mind. How do you feel? Can you go from one place to another, in your imagination if no other place?

If so, then you slide again. You go from the world of the second card to the world of the third card, and then again, until you are finally at your least-anxious card, a card that may indeed feel quite wonderful or may just be an improvement over the first card.

You can slide in real life, you know—not just on television programs or in your imagination. Sliding starts with one small step. Where are you now in your life, in reference to the four cards in front of you? If you are at any of the cards except for the final one, what is a concrete step that you can take in your life that will start you on your sliding adventure? Record it in your journal and resolve to begin sliding as soon as possible. Don't try to slide more than one card at a time, and don't formulate more than one concrete step at a time. Some slides are so difficult that it may take two concrete steps for you to truly slide from one place to another, but it can be done, and you can do it.

Watching Over Me

As those of you who have worked more than a few of these exercises know, I get my inspiration from various places, but often from songs. I'm not really into angels, although I have been learning more about them lately, but at the time I wrote this exercise, the song "Angels Watching Over Me" was going through my mind, so this exercise is based on the refrain from that song, "All night, all day, angels watching over me."

In many cultures and religious beliefs, there is a role, known by different names, but enough alike in each case to be an archetype. This is the role of the Watcher. Mostly, the Watcher just watches, but the watcher also loves us, and, if asked, will intervene in some way, sometimes by giving emotional or spiritual comfort and sometimes by actual physical aid.

Some names in different systems that might apply to this Watcher are Guardian Angel, Totem, Inner Guide, Higher Self, Spirit Guide, Patron Saint, Patron God or Goddess, Ancestor, Hero or Heroine, Fairy, Undine, Sylph, Master, Deva, and more. It could be the presence of your grandmother who died when you were a child. It could be an archangel. It could be a dragon. It could be an aspect of your subconscious. It could be a family member or godparent still living. Watchers come in many forms.

In whatever system is comfortable to you, think about your Watcher. Have you ever felt the presence of your Watcher? If so, what is your Watcher like? (Some people may feel connected to several Watchers. For the purposes of this exercise, choose one.) If you are unsure about a Watcher, be still, and ask your Watcher to make his or her presence known to you.

Thinking about your Watcher, go through your Tarot deck, faceup. (Record the name of your deck and thoughts about your Watcher in your Tarot journal.) Choose a card that seems to resonate with your concept of your Watcher. What is the card? How does it seem to fit your Watcher?

Go through your deck again. This time look for a card that seems to describe the relationship between you and your Watcher. (It may be the same card; it may be a different card.) What card is it, and how does it describe your relationship?

Be still, and be sensitive to the presence of your Watcher. Your Watcher's love for you is something that you can always count on. Your Watcher's wish for your growth and well-being is unconditional.

Ask your Watcher to send you a message through the Tarot. Shuffle your deck slowly, thinking on your Watcher and your Watcher's love for you. Fan your deck facedown on a flat surface. Let your hand hover over the cards until a card feels right. Choose that card, and turn it over. (All cards will be read upright for the purpose of this exercise.) What is it? What message do you get from your Watcher based on this card?

Based on this message, determine a specific action you can take in your life to affirm to yourself and your Watcher your acceptance of this message. Record it in your journal and then do it.

Tarot Pentacles Mandala

This is an exercise that I taught at Womongathering, June 1999. The theme grew out of a letter that I got several years ago from a friend who had been inspired by a book review. I've taken the basic concept and applied it to the suit of Pentacles.

Think of all of the things that the suit of Pentacles stands for: health, money, home, your body, the earth, work, prosperity, abundance, skills, the root chakra, survival, food, and more. Think of some of the physical symbols on Tarot cards that picture these concepts: disks, stones, shields, coins, houses, castles, mountains, planets, fields, the human body, fruit, grain, pregnant women, large animals, and more.

Choose a Tarot deck, and go through the deck, faceup, setting aside cards that represent, to you, all that you wish for on the physical and material plane. Many of these cards will be Pentacles, but you can also choose other cards as well. The Empress card, for example, is a very good example of a non-Pentacle card you might want to choose as representing physical plenty.

At this point, you may have a lot of cards. Take the cards you have chosen and shuffle them. Facedown, choose five. Turn those five over. List these cards in your Tarot journal. From each card, choose a symbol, something rather simple to duplicate—a heart, a circle, a star, a wave, a curve, a straight line, whatever. Draw those shapes. Study them. How do those symbols speak to you? What message do they give? Your artistic ability doesn't have to be great to be able to work with basic shapes and symbols.

From an artistic point of view, how can you combine those shapes in interesting ways? My friend Tonie took two curves, a small circle, and a straight line, and made a dancing stick woman. (The small circle was the head. One curve formed outstretched arms, the other dancing legs. The straight line became the trunk of the body.) She was very creative without needing a lot of artistic ability.

Draw a circle at least as big as a CD. You might want to use a plain white paper plate or, if you have paints, you might want to paint on the back of a spare CD/ROM, possibly one of those unwanted freebies that you get in the mail. Make a mandala for yourself using the symbols that you have chosen. Repeat the symbols as often as desired to make an interesting pattern. Tonie put her dancing stick woman in the center, and placed stars around the stick woman and waves under her so that her woman was dancing on the ocean. Tonie then made a circular border of hearts inside double crescents. Your mandala can be simpler or more complex than this.

Use your "Tarot Pentacles Mandala" as a meditation device. Keep it where you can see it several times a day. Use it for reflection and inspiration.

Make a record in your Tarot journal about the cards you chose, about the symbols you chose, and the mandala you made. Record your feelings, responses, thoughts, insights, and inspirations when you look at your mandala. Some people are surprised at the beauty they can create and also at the power of their mandala as a meditation tool.

The concept of making an actual mandala itself seems most congenial with the suit of Pentacles, but it can be applied to any of the other suits. If you have found using this mandala useful, you might also want to make a mandala for the other three suits of Tarot, especially if you are having issues with some of the areas represented by those suits.

Little Me

This is a very simple exercise, but one that packs a great deal of power if you do it honestly and thoroughly. It falls into the school of inner child work, although I'm using the term "little me" rather than "inner child."

Go through your deck, faceup, and choose a card that represents you as a child. Describe this card in your journal and tell how this card represents you as a child. Were you a shy child or an outgoing child? Were you serious or playful? Were you secure or insecure? How does this card reflect this? How is this card different from how you were as a child? If you could change your childhood, would you have been more or less like this card? In what ways?

Prop the card up in front of you. If you wish, you might also get out a photograph of yourself as a child and put it side by side with the card. If so, what, if any, similarities do you see between the card and the photograph of you as a child?

As an adult, have you lost anything from your childhood that you cherished? Innocence? Belief? Trust? Optimism? Confidence? If so, ask your "little me" (either in the card or the photograph) how you can get back what you have lost. What is the answer?

Do you as an adult have any message for your younger self? Is there anything you have learned over the years that would have helped you as a child? Is there some knowledge or a secret that you can share with your younger self that would have spared you much childhood agony? If so, tell the card and/or the photograph. What is that message? Did the "little me" in the card or photograph respond to your message? If so, how?

Based on this exercise, determine a concrete step to take that will help bring your adult self into better harmony with your "little me." What is this step? Do it—today, if possible, and no later than this week.

Chakra Dance

A general understanding of chakras is necessary in order to work this exercise. For those of you unfamiliar with chakras, please refer to Appendix A at the end of this book.

Choose a chakra that you want to work with. This will depend on who you are and what is going on with your life right now. Today, you may choose the solar plexus, but on another day, you might choose the crown chakra. Record in your Tarot journal which chakra you are going to work with and briefly tell what you would like changed about the energy of this chakra.

Choose your Tarot deck, recording it in your journal as well. Go through your Tarot deck, faceup. You are going to choose three cards. The first card is going to somehow (directly or indirectly) depict the state of your chosen chakra. This card doesn't have to emphasize or even show the chakra that you want to work on. What it needs to do is show how it feels to have the clogged or out-of-balance or problematic chakra. In other words, if you are having trouble with your root chakra, choose a card that, to you, seems to show someone or something with trouble with root chakra issues.

The second card that you choose will show very clearly the chakra that you want to work with. The card doesn't have to show the chakra in a positive position, but it does need to clearly show the chakra. You need to be able to clearly see the location of your chosen chakra on a person's body on this card.

The third card that you choose needs to show someone who has your chosen chakra working well, being clear, in balance, and in harmony. You don't need to be able to see the chakra on this card, but, again using the root chakra as an example, this card would show someone who, to you, has root chakra issues in good form, whose root chakra is functioning healthily and well.

Record the names of your three cards in your journal. Describe them briefly. Lay them out in a row, left to right. Look carefully at each card. As if you were a mime or taking an acting class, position your body like the person in the first card whose chakra is out of balance. How does it feel?

Position yourself like the person in the second card whose chakra is shown prominently. How does it feel? Position yourself like the person in the third card who exemplifies a healthy chakra? How does it feel?

Now, slowly, move gracefully from one pose to another, beginning with the first card and ending with the third card. Dance each card, and move from the first one to the second one to the third one, making a continuous dance of the three poses and movements. How did this movement feel? Can you feel any changes in your body as you move from one position to another? Make sure that you dance one continuous dance combining all three poses, rather than doing a separate dance for each card. You may want to repeat your dance several times in order to observe how you feel as you go from one pose to another. Record your feelings after you've danced.

Concrete step: *Do* the chakra dance, don't just visualize what it would be like if you were to do it.

My Champion

Sometimes these exercises are prompted by events in my own life, sometimes by movies I've seen or things in the news, and sometimes by personal requests that I get from others. This exercise was prompted by a personal e-mail request.

Everyone has times when she or he feels weak or powerless. Everyone has times when they are weak or powerless. Sometimes we just need to accept our weakness, our powerlessness—but at other times it would be great if we had a champion of some sort, a champion in the old-fashioned sense.

In medieval times, if someone could not fight for him- or herself, then a champion would fight on their behalf. I don't know about you, but I've often wished for a champion. These days my husband sometimes serves as my champion, and sometimes I serve as his champion as well. We take turns being champion for each other. However, there are times when I still feel in need of a champion for various reasons, so I really sympathized with the request for this exercise.

According to *Merriam Webster's Collegiate Dictionary*, a champion is a "warrior; fighter"; "a militant advocate or defender"; or "one that does battle for another's rights or honor."

Look through your Tarot deck, faceup. Which card would you choose as your champion? Record the card and the deck in your Tarot journal. This card might change from time to time, according to the circumstances of your life. If you don't currently feel in need of a champion, you might choose whichever champion you think you'd use the most in the future or one you would have used in the past.

Describe the card in your journal. How do you think that the figure in this card could serve as a good champion for you? What skills and strengths does the person have? How would you feel if you really had a person like this as a personal champion?

Remember the Native American saying, "If you give a person a fish, you feed him for a day. If you teach him to fish, you feed him for life." Quietly hold your card before you and visualize your Tarot champion in the room with you. Ask your champion to teach you to champion yourself. What does your champion say? What steps does your champion suggest that you take?

It may take time for you to learn the skills and strength to be your own champion. You may need extra help in the meantime, until you learn to fish for yourself, to be your own champion. Ask your Tarot champion to send a spiritual champion to be with you and to help you as well so that you will not be defenseless.

Each of us has strengths that we don't recognize. Ask your Tarot champion to help you see your own strengths and resources. Ask your Tarot champion to show you others that you may be able to turn to. What does your Tarot champion tell you?

If you have trouble getting a message from your Tarot champion, ask your champion to send you a message via your Tarot cards. Shuffle your deck and deal a card to represent your aid. What is the card? How could it be an aid for you?

Do you see the card representing your champion in the same way? Do you see yourself the same way? Record any changes or observations in your journal.

Resolve to do at least one of the steps suggested by your Tarot champion within the next twenty-four hours, if possible. What is that step?

Miracle

This exercise is loosely based on the song and music video by Mike and the Mechanics called "All I Need Is a Miracle." Sometimes, in life, we feel that a certain situation is hopeless, that if things were to get truly better, we would need a miracle. "Only a miracle can save me now," we think. Is there an area in your life that feels this way? If so, this exercise may prove helpful.

Look through your deck, face up, and find a card that most clearly says to you, "Here's your miracle." This card should represent the miracle that you feel you need, not describe the problem or issue at hand. Record in your Tarot journal the name of your miracle card, including the name of the deck that you are using. Why does this card say "miracle" to you? You can apply it to a particular situation where you feel you need a miracle or you can discuss the card more generally as a miracle card. For instance, although the Tower is not normally what we would consider a miracle card, in certain situations it might be the perfect miracle card. How does your card represent a miracle to you at the moment that you are doing this exercise?

Make a list of all of the positive attributes of your miracle card that come to mind. This list may be short, or it may be long. Which positive attributes of the miracle card seem most helpful to you? Why? Are there any positive attributes that you can draw on in your life? Are there any positive attributes you can work on developing in your life? For instance, if I had written "communication" as a positive attribute, how can I draw on that attribute in my own life? If I am not a good communicator, how can I learn to be a better communicator?

Can you think of anyone (personal acquaintance or celebrity or historical person) who seems to embody the miraculous qualities of your card? Who? How?

If you were to try and model yourself after this person, what would be the first step you would take toward transforming yourself into the positive attributes of your miracle card and your miracle role model? Make this step as concrete as possible, as detailed as possible, and make sure that it is something that you can actually do. Commit to taking that first step as soon as possible, within twenty-four hours, if possible. If it is not possible, break the first step into mini-steps, and take the first mini-step. Keep your miracle card out in a conspicuous place to help inspire you as you become your own miracle worker.

Nightmare

This exercise, like many of the other exercises, works best if you don't read ahead to the end. Choose a card that makes you extremely uncomfortable. No one card is totally positive or totally negative, and I don't mean to put value judgments on cards. However, when all is said and done, some cards do make us more uncomfortable than others. Choose a card that most resembles your personal nightmares. Record the card and deck in your Tarot journal.

What about the card makes you uncomfortable? Why?

Choose the name of a friend or relative, someone close to you, someone you really care about in a nonjudgmental way. Tell a brief story about your friend based on the picture in the card.

For instance, if I had chosen the 10 of Swords in the *Hanson-Roberts* deck (similar to *Rider-Waite-Smith*), I could say, "Sue was on her way to a mountain retreat for a time of study and meditation. Along the way, she was set upon by bandits who robbed her and stabbed her repeatedly, leaving her alone in the wasteland. As she lay on the ground, in a pool of her own blood, her beaded necklace scattered, she continued to struggle slowly, thinking that if she could only make it to the foot of the mountains, the holy people there would find her and save her."

You will reach a point in your uncomfortable card where you may be unsure of where to go next. Does your friend die? Does she get miraculously saved by a pack of wolves? It's your call. Whatever you think will happen, let it happen. This is your friend, and you decide what she/he would do. There should, however, be some logic to what happens.

In other words, for that pack of wolves to be a means of salvation, your friend should be experienced with working with wild animals. The story does not have to be probable, only possible. In other words, it can have only a 0.02 percent of probability, but if it's possible, it can happen. In my story, an example of an impossibility would be for the mountains to miraculously move to Sue just because she wishes to be at the foot of the mountains. A possibility that might be improbable would be that a wise person in the mountains looks through a telescope and sees Sue and rushes to her aid. This is your friend. Make up the story. It can be sad or happy, but it should suit your relationship with your friend and your friend's character.

How do you feel about your story? Do you feel sad? Do you judge your friend in any way, based on this story? Has he or she failed you or anyone else in any way in this story? Is there anything else that your friend could have possibly done in this situation to make things better? Has this given you any insights into your friend or your friendship? If so, what? Record the answers to all of these questions in your Tarot journal.

Now, tell the story again, only this time, let the story be about you. You are the main character. The story is the same; only the main character has changed, from your friend to you.

How did the story feel this time? (Note: The emphasis is on feeling.) Do you feel sad? Do you feel relief? Do you judge yourself in any way? Is your reaction to the story being about you different from your reaction to the story being about your friend? If so, what does this tell you? If not, what does this tell you?

Do you see the card in the same manner? If not, how has this exercise changed how you see the card? No concrete step for this exercise.

Life Purpose

What is your purpose in life? Often, we don't really know. The Tarot can be useful in helping you to discover your life purpose. Before you begin, you should be aware that life purpose and goals are not the same thing. Goals are individual ways to fulfill a life purpose. Concrete steps are actions that help us fulfill goals.

Your life purpose is a thread in your life that describes (with many detours for some of us!) the whole thread of your life. If at life's end, you could sum up your whole life in one sentence or phrase, it might be your life purpose.

Some examples might be:

- To show love and compassion for the downtrodden
- To teach people to notice the divine in everyday life
- To mend fences
- To teach a person or group of persons
- To inspire a person or group of persons
- To entertain a person or group of persons
- To teach entertainingly
- To delight the weary
- To brighten a person or neighborhood
- To heal a person or community
- To teach a special topic
- To transform a ghetto
- To inspire a town
- To encourage a neighborhood

Your life purpose may sound very corny when you put it into words. Don't worry if it does. Sometimes things sound corny because they are true, simple, essential, and powerful. "I love you" is corny, but it is one of the most true, simple, essential, and powerful statements in the world.

For instance, your life purpose could be inspiring others by teaching about the past. There are many ways that you could do this, many goals that would achieve this purpose—being a school teacher, being an author, being an archaeologist, or even being a filmmaker, if your name is Steven Spielberg.

You could have as a life purpose to delight and thrill people by your physical skills. To fulfill this life purpose, you could use many different occupations or hobbies as goals—you could be a local part-time clown, a street mime, or high-school track team member, a dancer, an action movie star, or even an Olympic athlete, if your name is Dorothy Hamill.

You are going to focus in this exercise on finding your life purpose. Some of you already know your life purpose; some of you do not. For those who already do, it is still helpful to identify your life purpose with a Tarot card so that you have a visual image of your life purpose. You are not going to look at goals to help you achieve your life's purpose at this time.

Think carefully about different values and desires in your life. Think about them in groups. Do you see any trends? Any common elements? Any uniting purpose or theme?

As you think about your values and desires in life, with an eye toward a life purpose, look through your deck faceup. Put aside any cards that seem to resonate for you. When you've gone through your entire deck, go through the cards you've put aside a second time. Do you see any themes or common components, symbols, or objects in the cards you've put aside? If so, what does this say to you?

As you go through the deck, thinking and looking, jot down thoughts that may come to you. Do not censor yourself for impracticality or self-criticism. Life purposes seem to sound rather grand and pompous. It is when we combine individual goals with the life purpose that we have something that approaches reality and normality. I mean, can you imagine young Steven Spielberg saying, "I'm going to grow up to inspire others by teaching them about the past," or young Dorothy Hamill saying, "I'm going to grow up to delight and thrill people by my physical skills." However, if young Steven Spielberg had said, "I'm going to direct and produce movies," or young Dorothy Hamill had said, "I'm going to be an ice skater," we still might have smiled indulgently, but we would have had a different internal reaction. These are goals, and we have clear mental pictures of people achieving these goals.

For example, Steven Spielberg might choose the Hermit, the Magician, the Wheel of Fortune, the Tower, the King of Swords, the King of Pentacles, the Queen of Cups, the Queen of Wands, the 4 of Pentacles, and the 6 of Pentacles as possible life-purpose cards. Dorothy Hamill might choose the Page of Swords, the Page of Wands, the World, the Star, the Sun, the Ace of Wands, and the Chariot as possible life-purpose cards.

Narrow down your life-purpose card choices to four to six cards. What cards are they? Record them in your Tarot journal. If you feel that you already know your life's purpose, record how these cards relate to this purpose. Give concrete examples from the images on the cards themselves rather than textbook meanings of the cards. Do you have any surprises or new insights into your life purpose from looking at these cards and from choosing them?

If you don't already know your life's purpose, look through the cards that have spoken to you. Do you see any themes in common? Any messages? Any ideals? How can you distill one message from the individual messages of the cards? For instance, if you have chosen the Empress, the Moon, the 9 of Pentacles, the Queen of Pentacles, the Ace of Pentacles, and the World, you might see some common symbols of outdoors, gardens, being a good steward of the earth, nurturing, and communing with Nature. You might therefore decide on a tentative life purpose of nurturing the earth and inspiring others to do the same.

Note of clarification: When people have done this exercise, they've tended to pick goals rather than life purposes. Life purpose is more universal than a goal. Your life purpose can be a constant throughout your life, but you can have many goals at different times in your life which will all help to fulfill your life's purpose. Often, people confuse goals with a concrete step, and I tell them, "Get more specific!" This time, I want you to be less specific in your thinking, more general, more universal.

Let me simplify the steps of this exercise.

Go through your deck faceup, looking for cards that reflect the desires and inspirations of your life. Narrow your selection down to four to six cards. Look for common themes, symbols, and ideas in these cards. Record these.

From these themes, symbols, and ideals, can you find an overall message that might be your life purpose (not a goal)? If so, record it. If you already feel you know your life purpose, how do the cards you have chosen reflect your life purpose? Record your impressions.

There is no concrete step in this exercise, but I want to suggest that you reread your journal entries on this one at six month intervals and make changes and updates to your entry.

I Gotta Be Me

This is one of the longest and most complicated of the exercises, but also one of the most popular ones. It is extremely ambitious and draws on both numerology and astrology. You will want to consult Appendix B for astrological background information and charts of correspondences.

Some people who like to do these Tarot for self-discovery exercises may not know their astrological information or may not be interested in working with astrology. For astrological skeptics, it is fine to be skeptical. My basic guideline is to test each new metaphysical tool. I ask myself the following questions: Is it helpful? Is it useful? Does it make sense? Does it inspire? If the answers are yes, I proceed. If the answers are no, then I put that tool aside for the time being. You don't have to believe in astrology in order to find this exercise helpful, useful, and inspiring. I don't really believe in *Personality* and *Soul* cards, but I find them helpful, useful, and inspiring. It doesn't take much astrological knowledge to do the exercise. All you really need to know is your Sun sign, your Moon sign, and your Rising sign (the sign on your Ascendant).

That said, for those who want to try "I Gotta Be Me," please consult Appendix B if you are astrologically challenged. In addition, in order to do this exercise, you'll need a copy of your natal chart. You can get free charts on the internet at a number of places, or you can order an astrological chart from Llewellyn for a very modest price.

For those brave souls among you whom I have not scared away, please begin. Make sure you read this exercise thoroughly and understand it before attempting it. If this exercise does not appeal to you, just skip it and go on to another exercise. There are plenty in this book to choose from.

To begin, you will need to calculate your personality and soul cards and you will also need to know your Sun sign, Moon sign, and the sign on your Ascendant. According to Mary Greer in *Tarot for Your Self* and *Tarot Constellations*, the personality card indicates life purposes, aspirations, and lessons to be learned. The soul card indicates soul purpose and qualities that will assist us. To find your personality card, add your month, day, and year of birth. Make sure that you have included the year in your calculations.

You should end up with something like this:

$$11$$
$$15$$
$$\underline{1954}$$
$$1980$$

Then, take each digit from your total, and add them:

$$1 + 9 + 8 + 0 = 18$$

If the number is greater than 22, add those digits together. This is your personality number. It has a corresponding card in the Major Arcana, going by the number on the card. Take this card, and add the digits again if they are double digits ($1 + 8 = 9$). This is your soul card number. It too has a Major Arcana card. In my own example, I have the Moon as my personality card and the Hermit as my soul card.

Sometimes this system can be a bit disconcerting at first glance. For instance, what if you got a *bad* card for one of your cards? Who wants the Tower or the Devil as a soul or personality card? You could either forget about this system (which isn't necessary for personal growth or for Tarot mastery) or you could find a way to deal with it by meditating on it and learning to find positive meaning in it.

To find out more about soul and personality cards, I recommend that you read Mary Greer's *Tarot for Your Self* and also her *Tarot Constellations*. Remember, the personality card indicates life purposes, aspirations, and lessons to be learned. The soul card indicates soul purpose and qualities that will assist us.

Think of this as an exercise, a challenge. Brainstorm. For me, the importance is not so much that I make the personality card and soul card fit me as that, by studying the cards and by reflecting on myself, I learn more about the cards and about myself. And isn't that what we're all here for anyway? We contain elements of all seventy-eight cards. By using numerology, some of the cards will have more significance for us. Personality and soul cards are just two of many numerologically significant cards. Some of you may find some cards to be more significant to you than others.

I find that it is useful to look at the personality and soul cards in combination with the cards that correspond to our Sun, Moon, and Ascendant. I have Sun in Scorpio (Death), Moon in Leo (Strength), and Ascendant in Cancer (Chariot). I'm a Moon/Hermit according to a numerological breakdown of my birthdate.

Astrologer Steven Forrest says that it is important for us to *feed* each part of our natal chart. We have to pay attention to all parts of it, particularly the big three of Sun, Moon, and Ascendant. He says that if you don't, you are setting yourself up for big time trouble. I've seen that in my own life. At times, I've ignored my Leo Moon and paid too much attention to my Cancer Ascendant. When I did so, I was very unhappy and depressed. I can't ignore my Cancer Ascendant either, so my goal is to find a way of life that will allow all parts of my chart to find healthy, creative, enriching expression.

If we take this and apply it to Tarot, then we could say that we have the goal to take our numerologically and astrologically special cards (for me: Death, Chariot, Strength, Moon, and Hermit) and see how we use them in our lives. Then we could ask questions, such as, "How can I better use these cards in my life? Do I need to draw more on these cards in my life? Do I need a better balance or mix between these cards in my life? How does the combination of these cards help me to better understand myself?" The "I Gotta Be Me" exercise is an attempt to help you find a way to strike this balance in your own life.

Laying the cards out as directed below can help us to find the answer to these questions.

1 Life Purpose = personality card

2 Companion or Helper = soul card

3 Doorway to the World = Ascendant card (card corresponding to sign on your Ascendant, your Rising sign card)

4 Personal Essence = Sun card (card corresponding to your Sun sign)

5 Individual Needs and Insecurities = Moon card (card corresponding to the sign of your Moon)

If you lay them out in a five-pointed star, card 1 (your Personality card representing life purpose) would be at the left *foot* of the card. Card 2 (your soul card representing your companion or helper) would be at the right *foot* of the card. Card 3 (your Ascendant card, representing your doorway to the world) would be at the left *hand*. Card 4 (your Sun card, representing your personal essence) would be at the *head* or *crown*. Card 5 (your Moon card, representing your individual needs and insecurities) would be at your right *hand*. You could lay out your five cards, look at them, and meditate on them. Then, you could go another step and write it up this way:

1 Life Purpose = the Moon

2 Companion or Helper = the Hermit

3 Doorway to the World = the Chariot

4 Personal Essence = Death

5 Individual Needs and Insecurities = Strength

The Rising Sign reflects how we see the world and how the world sees us. This is why I call the Ascendant card the "Doorway to the World" card. Our Sun sign is our real essence, who we are at the core. There are many different ways, however, for this essence to manifest itself in our lives. Not all Leos are the same, for instance. The Moon indicates our needs and insecurities, among other things.

Lay out your five cards. How do they describe you? How does this description not describe you? Would you like to be more like this layout? If so, how and why? Enter the answers to all of these questions in your Tarot journal.

Is there a lesson in these cards that helps you to understand yourself, how you see the world, who you really are, and what your needs are? Tell this lesson. What concrete action can you take as a result of your insights?

Many times, people will ask me to read for babies or for small children. Although I enjoy reading for children, unless a child is old enough to enjoy a reading, I prefer to do only mini-readings or abbreviated readings. However, I do find that this layout makes a very good gift for a newborn or a birthday gift for the parents of a small child. I hand color the cards and mount them on nice paper. The family has a nice visual picture of the child's personality. This also makes a nice gift to give to family and friends for special occasions.

Let My Sun Shine

For this exercise you will need at least two different Tarot decks. What is your Sun sign (the sign that the Sun was in when you were born)? Choose a card from each deck which corresponds to your Sun sign. This exercise will probably work best if you choose decks which have fairly different pictures on your Sun sign card. Choose your two (or three) decks. What are they?

(See Appendix B for one system of correspondences. Feel free to use your own preferred system of correspondences if you have one. Some decks have their own unique system of correspondences, and if you use one of those decks for this exercise, you will want to follow its system.)

Study each card carefully. How does each card help you to better understand yourself and your Sun sign? Questions you might want to consider as you study and think might include:

- How does the name of this card reveal something about my inner nature?

- How does the name of this card reveal something about my spiritual goals?

- How does the central figure on this card reveal a secret about my core essence?

- What is the central figure doing? How does this help me to understand my personal goals?

- What are other figures in the deck doing? How does this help me to understand my personal goals?

- What is the primary mood of this card? How does that reflect or fail to reflect my own primary mood?

- What colors predominate on this card? How does this reflect or fail to reflect my own color preferences?

- How do I see this card? What is the meaning of this card to me? How does this help me to understand myself? How well does this card describe me? How does this card fail to describe me? How is this card misleading about me?

After you have gone through these questions or similar ones that may occur to you, answer these questions or others which you feel moved to ask:

- Which version of my Sun sign card do I prefer? Why?

- Which version of my Sun sign card paints the most accurate portrait of who I am? Why?

- Which version of my Sun sign card is the most misleading about me? Why?

- Which version of my Sun sign card most closely matches how I see myself? Why?

- Which version of my Sun sign card do I most want to grow most like? Why?

- Which version of my Sun sign card inspires me most? Why?

- Which version of my Sun sign card most reflects my personal goals? Why?

Based on a personal goal reflected in one of the cards, choose a concrete step to take which will help you to achieve one of your goals. What is that specific, concrete step? When will you do it?

My Lunar Consciousness

Most of the exercises in this book have fairly clear objectives. A few of them, like My Lunar Consciousness, are more vague and open-ended. There is no clear objective. The objective is to become attuned to your lunar consciousness and to record that attunement. There is no hidden agenda, nothing beyond that. However, if done with sensitivity and attention, this can be a very enlightening exercise.

Like the "I Gotta Be Me" exercise, "My Lunar Consciousness" relies on astrology. It uses astrology in a different way, however. Again, you do not have to be very knowledgeable in astrology to do this exercise. You should find all of the information that you need in Appendix B of this book. Getting set up to work this exercise is a bit ambitious, but the exercise itself is very simple.

In Tarot, several different cards are normally associated with the Moon: under the Golden Dawn tradition, with the High Priestess; by name, the Moon card; by astrological sign, the Chariot, because the Chariot is associated with Cancer, and the astrological sign Cancer is ruled by the Moon. It can also be associated with the Hierophant because the Hierophant is associated with Taurus, and the Moon is exalted in Taurus. Visually, many different cards have pictures of the Moon on them. In the *Rider-Waite-Smith* deck, for instance, there is a Moon on the 8 of Cups and on the 2 of Swords.

In addition, on any given day, the transiting Moon is in a sign. On Wednesday, August 9, 2000, the Moon was in Sagittarius, for example. One way to relate to the Moon on that day might have been to think about the sign of Sagittarius. In the Golden Dawn system, Sagittarius is associated with Temperance. Also, the Moon was in a specific sign at the moment of your birth. On the day that I was born, the Moon was in Leo. According to the Golden Dawn system, Leo is associated with Strength.

Some people like to associate the Waxing Moon with the Star or High Priestess (as representing the Maiden phase of the Moon), the Empress as the Full Moon (or Mother), and the Moon card as the waning phase of the Moon (crone or hag). So, right away, we have several different ways to associate the Moon with Tarot—various systems of associations and correspondences, the transiting Moon's sign, the sign of the Moon in a person's birth (natal) chart, phases of the Moon, and also visual representations of the Moon on the cards.

According to astrology, the Moon is positively associated with secure feelings and emotions, perceptive intuition and inner self, subconscious reflection and sensitivity, mother and the positive past. Neutrally, it is associated with the unconscious, the subconscious, the soul, reflection, fertility, memories, moods, and sensitivity. Negatively, the Moon is associated with out-of-control moodiness, cloudy intuition, excessive neediness, insecure feelings and emotions, living in the past, and insecurities. It rules the sign of Cancer and is exalted in Taurus. It is in its detriment in Capricorn and in its fall in Scorpio.

Thinking about the astrological description of the Moon, decide on one facet of the Moon to concentrate on. You could choose sensitivity or your mother, or living in the past or whatever. Choose one facet that appeals to you at this moment. You can do this exercise again at a later date, choosing a different facet, so choose just one facet at this time. If you are familiar with astrology, you can choose your own lunar facet to focus on, even one that isn't on my short list. Record the facet you have chosen in your Tarot journal.

Choose your Tarot deck, and go through your deck to find cards that seem to you to feel like the facet of the Moon you have chosen. You may choose cards with pictures of the Moon on them or not. You may choose cards that have systematic or astrological correspondences to the Moon or not. Go with the whims of the moment. Remember, you can always do the exercise again later with another choice.

Spread the choices out in front of you. Look at them carefully. Which one most closely seems to resonate with the facet of the Moon you have chosen? Choose it. If you have trouble deciding, turn your choices over, mix them up, and then randomly choose from among your choices. Record your choice.

According to the Golden Dawn system, the color of the Moon is blue. Other people like to use silver or gray for the Moon. Choose a color that, to you, represents the Moon.

At this point, you will need to ready your space for meditation. You might want to turn off your phone, light some incense, dim your lights, tell your family to leave you alone for a little bit, whatever you do when you want to meditate. Sit comfortably in your favorite meditation position. Put your Tarot card where you can see it. Study it carefully. Try to mentally imprint the card on your consciousness.

Begin to breathe slowly and calmly. If you have a regular routine for going into meditation, you may use that. If you don't, just try to breathe slowly and to calm yourself. Picture yourself surrounded by an aura of colored light, the color that you have chosen to represent the Moon. Let the light extend at least six inches out in every direction.

Then, mentally levitate your Tarot card so that it is in front of you and *grow* it until it is about the same size as you. Picture it also surrounded by an aura of your chosen color. Gradually let your card become more and more realistic, until you can see the characters move and breathe. Let the action *roll* like a movie screen. Don't try to direct the action—just watch. What happens?

After a few moments (after significant action or a period of disintegration or stagnation), gradually lower the card and shrink the auras. Concentrate strongly on being in your physical body in the here and now. Give a strong and forceful exhale, saying, "Hua."

Record what happened in your meditation in your journal. You will want to be able to go back and reread this later, so include as many details as possible. This meditation might be simple; it might be complex. It might have great meaning and impact; it might have little meaning or impact. Record it nonetheless.

The concrete step for this exercise is the same for everyone. As soon as possible after doing this exercise, try to go outside and observe the Moon. What phase is the Moon in? What does it look like? Does it feel any different? Do you get any additional insights from observing the Moon? If so, what are they?

Transition

There are many kinds of transition in life: birth, death, marriage, divorce, graduation, relocation, changing jobs, children leaving home, children moving back in, changes in spiritual path, redecoration of your home, and more. Some transitions are sudden; others are gradual. Some transitions are looked for; others are dreaded. No matter what kind of transition a person is undergoing, there is stress, and there will have to be adjustment. This exercise is about dealing with the stress of transition and learning to adjust to the changes in your life.

Choose your Tarot deck. Record it and the other pertinent information in your Tarot journal. Think of a change that you are currently going through or are about to go through. It could be a pleasant change or an unpleasant change, or have both pleasant and unpleasant qualities. For instance, at the time I originally wrote this exercise, my daughter Mary Frances was about to graduate from high school and go off to college. In some ways, this was a very joyous occasion. In other ways, it was fearful. Write about this change, just enough to get your ideas on paper. You may write more, of course, if you choose to. Some changes need a lot of explanation. Other changes need very little.

Go through your deck faceup. Choose a card that seems to objectively show the change you are going through most accurately. Now, go through your deck faceup again. This time, choose a card which seems to best picture your feelings about this change. This second card doesn't need to have anything to do with the change itself, but it should relate to your feelings.

In other words, if you are feeling insecure, you might choose the 2 of Pentacles. If you are feeling caught between a rock and a hard place, you might choose the 2 of Swords. Neither might relate obviously to your first card. Or, they can relate very obviously. Choose whatever works best for you.

Why did you chose the cards that you did? How do they picture your change and your feelings about that change?

Change is a process. There is a beginning, a middle, and an end to change, or at least to a stage of change. What stage of change are you currently in? You might be pre-beginning if you have chosen something that is to happen in the future. No matter what stage of change you are in, you can still make changes to the ending, even if you are in the ending. Where would you like to be, emotionally, spiritually, and physically, at the end of this change?

Choose a Tarot card that best shows where you'd like to be at the end of the change. Be at least somewhat realistic. For example, if your change is that someone important to you has died, do not choose a card showing him or her coming back to you in this lifetime. This will not happen, no matter how much you want it to happen. However, you could show a card to represent being joined again in the afterlife or in a future life, or you could choose a card that showed someone new coming into your life or a card to show you being happy and strong on your own again.

Write about this Tarot card. Explain how it pictures where you'd like to be at the end of this change. Now, turn your deck over. Shuffle. You are going to concentrate on an aid that will help you successfully achieve your chosen end to this change. Randomly choose a card, facedown, in whatever manner is most comfortable to you. (You can shuffle, cut, and deal a card off the top; fan the cards out and choose a card to which you feel drawn; or any other method that appeals to you of choosing a card without looking.) What is this card? How do you interpret it as an aid in your quest for a successful transition?

Concrete step time. In order to successfully navigate your transition, what is one concrete step you can take now, today, that will help you? Be specific. Be timely. And, don't forget to do it once you've decided on it.

A Spirituality of My Own

This exercise bears some similarities to "Lost in the Wasteland" on page 72. You may also want to refer to that exercise.

For many of us, there is a point in our lives where the spirituality of our childhood or early adulthood no longer seems to work for us. We are still spiritual persons, but the spirituality that we have been practicing doesn't feel right anymore. At such times, we may find ourselves in a spiritual void. We know what doesn't work for us, but we don't know where to go, where to look, how to find out what will work. For some people, the experience is even more intense, and they undergo what is sometimes called the dark night of the soul, or the great abyss.

At such points, we may be like the Fool. If you are at a spiritual void or crossroads or abyss, or if you have experienced such a time in your life, you may find this exercise useful. This exercise uses the technique of automatic drawing and writing, an effective means, like Tarot, of conveying messages from the subconscious mind to the conscious mind.

Choose your Tarot deck and record it in your Tarot journal. Pull out the Fool card in this deck, and tell how this card describes you at your spiritual void (past or present).

Go through your deck, faceup, and choose one to three cards that describe your past spirituality. Tell what those cards are and describe how those cards reflect your past spirituality.

Go through your deck again, with the cards faceup. Choose one to three cards that seem to picture what you want in your future spirituality. This might be rather hazy. If so, that's okay. Tell the names of the cards, but at this time do not describe them, and do not describe how they relate to what you want.

Put the card(s) for future spirituality before you. Have a pen and paper handy. Look at the card(s) carefully. As you look at the card(s), let your mind slowly unfocus and go into a half-dream state, where you go when you daydream. Take your pen in hand, and let words or images pour out. For some of you, images will come, and you'll make little sketches. For others of you, words will come. Don't censor. Whatever comes, comes.

When you are done with the automatic writing/automatic drawing, put the pen down, and look at what you've written or drawn. Summarize it. (You can edit yourself at this stage, but do not edit yourself during the automatic flow.)

How does the automatic writing or drawing relate to the Tarot card(s)? What guidance do you get for your future spirituality from the card(s) and/or writing or drawing?

Look at your Fool card. Take the card representing your current or past spirituality (if you've used more than one, at this point, narrow your choice to one). Take the card representing the future direction that you'd like for your spirituality (if you've used more than one, at this point, narrow your choice to one). Place the three cards in a row: Past Spirituality, Fool, Future Spirituality. You are at the Fool point right now (unless you are looking at an event in your past).

What action could the Fool take to move him closer to his Future Spirituality? What concrete step can you take in your own life to move you closer to your Future Spirituality? Set a specific time for taking this step and resolve to do it. If it's helpful, first devise an overall goal and then decide on a concrete step to help you fulfill that goal.

Lessons from Misfortune

I don't know about the rest of you, but I can do without any further misfortune in my life. I would just as soon have no more illness, accidents, losses, pain, hurt, betrayal, or disappointment. As they say here in the South, "It ain't gonna happen," but I wish that it would. It is said that we can learn from pain or from joy. I choose joy, but, in the meantime, whenever I get pain, I'm definitely going to try and learn from it. If I don't learn from pain, then I've experienced it wastefully. Might as well get something good out of something painful, right?

Here is an exercise for learning from misfortune. It started out as an exercise in learning from illness, but then I thought, "Why not expand it for anything that we might consider unpleasant?" Why not indeed?

Before you begin the exercise, before you choose your topic, look carefully at the word "misfortune." It means, "an event or conjunction of events that causes an unfortunate or distressing result; bad luck." Be careful not to expand the concept of the exercise into "Lessons from Unhappiness" or "Lessons from Pain." This is not what the exercise is for. It can work that way, but there are other exercises that work better for unhappiness or that might work better for the reason behind the unhappiness. So, choose your exercise carefully. The first exercise you come to is not necessarily the best one for what you want to achieve.

It is my most earnest hope that by learning from misfortune and by making inward and outward changes in my life based on what I've learned, I'll have less misfortune. At least that's the theory. If I don't end up with less misfortune, at the very least I'll end up with more enlightenment, and more enlightenment is never anything to ignore.

It is best to do this exercise as you go, not reading to the end before beginning. Choose your Tarot deck, recording it and other important information in your Tarot journal. Think of something in your life (current or recent past) that might be thought of as unfortunate or unpleasant: illness, accident, disappointment, hurt, distress, or loss. Record briefly what this event or situation is.

Think carefully about this event or situation. For the purposes of this exercise, put aside all thoughts of, "Why did this happen to me?" and all thoughts of guilt, blame, or judgment. These thoughts have no purpose here.

Go through your Tarot deck, faceup, and choose the card that describes the situation or event most closely. Do not pick a card that shows your feelings about the event or situation or even society's views. Be very literal here. Have you been ill? Then you might pick a card showing someone at rest—sitting or lying down. Have you been in an accident? Then maybe you should pick a card showing someone with a bandage. Have you had a loss? Then choose a card showing someone weeping.

Look at this card very closely. Choose a character in the card that you feel most represents the situation (if there is more than one character). Tell about the card and about the character, and about how they fit the situation or event.

Choose two to three objects on the card (a cup, a tree, a star, a cloud). Describe these objects. (This is to get you really looking at the card.) How does the character that you've chosen relate to each of these objects? Does he or she see them at all? Does he or she hold them? Could any of the objects prove helpful to the person in his or her situation? If so, how?

Ask the question, "What is a helpful lesson for this character to learn from his or her situation?" Then, choose a card from your deck face down. (You can choose a card in any way that is comfortable to you, as long as you do it without looking at the cards.) Turn the card over. What is it?

What helpful lesson might this card have for the character in your first card? An answer may come to you very quickly, or it may take a bit of thought and contemplation. Study the card carefully, looking at body posture, facial expressions, and various objects in the card. What hints of the lesson can you get from these components?

Now, using this second card as your resource, ask the question, "What can I learn from my situation?" Record your answer.

Taking your answer, determine a goal (new or renewed) for your life. Based on that goal, then determine a concrete step that you can take in your life which will incorporate that lesson into your being.

Tower Survivor

Some things will mark us for life, and no exercise, no matter how inspired, is going to erase all pain, nor should any exercise do so. However, what an exercise *can* do is to help is to take our pain and either release it or channel it into something useful or something that we can learn. We are going to have pain in life, sometimes devastating pain. This is part of the human condition. But when pain enters our lives, we have a choice about what to do with the pain. Whenever possible, I try to learn and grow from the pain. I do not wish pain on myself in order that I might learn and grow, but when I get pain, I figure that I might see how I can turn the pain into an opportunity for growth and service to others.

So, this exercise is designed to help us deal with what Tarotists call Tower experiences. Tower experiences do not normally have physical towers as a component, but the September 11, 2001, plane crashes into the World Trade Center towers were vivid reminders that sometimes the Tarot cards can be interpreted quite literally. Tower experiences include deaths in the family, divorce, losing your job, going bankrupt, a fire, becoming disabled, a severe accident, a sudden move, actually any sudden change. Normally, we think of negative or painful sudden changes, but the Tower can also represent sudden changes that turn out positively.

Have a recent "Tower" experience in mind. This experience can be something worldwide or it can be something personal, affecting only you. What is your Tower experience? Why does it feel like a Tower experience to you?

Choose your Tarot deck. What is it? Go through your deck, faceup, and pull the Tower card. Study the card. How does the picture on this card illustrate your particular experience?

Take a piece of blank paper. Sketch out the bare essentials of your Tower card but making changes to more specifically reflect your personal experience. Don't worry about the quality of the art. Use stick figures and chunky boxes if you like, Use whatever medium you have handy—ink, pencil, crayons. Do this quickly.

Where are you on your Tower sketch? If you didn't draw yourself originally, put yourself in the picture now. If you need to, draw yourself on a separate piece of paper and glue or tape yourself into the previous picture.

Put your sketch aside. Go through your Tarot deck and pull the Judgement card. Judgement represents resurrection, rising from the ashes. In the *Robin Wood* deck, in fact, we see a phoenix in the background, rising from the flames. Using the Judgement card as a loose inspiration, draw another quick sketch of yourself either rising from a watery grave or rising from ashes or flames. In this sketch, the emphasis should be on *you*, the survivor, and not on the Tower experience itself. Do not draw a tower on this sketch at all.

Go through your deck a third time. This time, look for a card that says to you "survivor." This card will be different for you at different times of your life and may also be different for you depending on which Tarot deck you are using. What card have you chosen? What does it look like? Why does it say "survivor" to you?

You are going to make a third sketch. Again, quickly, draw out the bare basics of this card, but this time, put your face and body type in the place of the survivor character on your card.

At this point, I am going to suggest a modest ritual. Light some incense and some candles. I would suggest five candles, one for each of the four directions and one for the center. You can put them all on one tray or plate, arranged in the shape of an equal-armed cross if you like. You should also have a fireproof dish handy and a container of water.

Light your center candle first, and then the other four candles, beginning with the east and going clockwise. When you've finished, be very still, very quiet. Say either to yourself or out loud, "Like the force that split the Tower, I have been torn apart." Then, take your Tower sketch, tear it apart, and set both halves aflame from your center candle. Drop it into the fireproof dish. Be careful not to spread sparks or to let your sleeves catch on fire.

Next, pick up your sketch based on the Judgement card. Say, "I consecrate myself to the flames so that I may rise from the ashes." Carefully, light your Judgement sketch from your center candle and let it burn in your fireproof dish.

Finally, pick up your survivor sketch. Say, "I am a survivor. I have been through the flames and am purified, tempered, and strengthened by my ordeal." Take your survivor sketch and hold it high over each candle, saying, in turn, "I am a survivor of the flame of the east. I am a survivor of the flame of the south. I am a survivor of the flame of the west. I am a survivor of the flame of the north. I am a survivor of the primal flame." Be careful not to let this sketch catch fire.

Wave your sketch through the smoke of your incense, saying, "Let this sweet aroma further consecrate me." Put a finger into the container of water. Let a drop of water drip from your finger onto the survivor sketch, saying, "Purified by fire, consecrated by air, I am now reborn through water." Using another a drop of water, anoint yourself on your crown or forehead.

At this point, snuff out your candles. Your ritual is done. (The survivor sketch itself is a representative of earth. If you prefer, you can also rub salt on your sketch to represent earth.)

Afterward, if you like, you may turn your rough survivor sketch into a more polished work of art and place it in a special place to remind yourself that you are a survivor.

What action can you take to show that you are a survivor of the Tower? Resolve to take that action as soon as possible. If it cannot be done soon, do a preliminary step towards the action or perform a symbolic act that represents it.

Visiting the World of If

Sometimes songs get stuck in my head. If you've read several previous exercises in this book, you've probably noted a lot of musical references in my exercises and comments. One morning, an odd little song from the musical *Gypsy* got stuck there, "If Mama Was Married." That song started me thinking about the concept of "if." I remembered other "if" songs: "If I Only Had a Brain" from *The Wizard of Oz* and "If" ("If a picture paints a thousand words, then why can't I paint you?") recorded by Bread.

"If" is a very powerful word and also a potentially destructive word. If we live too much in the world of if, we become like the person in the 7 of Cups (*Rider-Waite-Smith* version), full of imagination and wonder, but never actually getting anything done. It is a fantastic place, a great place, but it is not a place for living, only a place for visiting. Even when our "World of If" is positive, we endanger ourselves if we live too much there. Many young women become trapped in a special version of the "World of If" called, "Some day my prince will come." They delay their lives, waiting on their prince. Many of us spend far too long in other special variations of this world called, "Some day. . . ."

Some "Worlds of If" are rather negative, dwelling on the past, not the future, with accusations and blame: "If only I/you'd get a job, lose weight, finish school. . . ." Other "Worlds of If" are nostalgic: "If only I could go back to high school or college or when the kids were babies," or whatever.

Each of us has our own personalized "World of If." You may have more than one. What does your "World of If" look like? Is it a forward-looking "World of If" or a backward-looking one? Choose a Tarot deck and record it in your journal. Go through your deck, face-up, examining the cards closely. What Tarot card most fits your "World of If"? Why? (If you have more than one "World of If," you may choose a card for each world.) How does this "World of If" help you? How can staying too long in this "World of If" hurt you?

In the movie of *The Wizard of Oz*, the Scarecrow sang, "If I only had a brain," but it was obvious to all that he really had a brain.

Likewise, the Tin Man had a heart and the Cowardly Lion had courage, even though they didn't realize that they had them. Think of your own "World of If" again. Look at your "World of If" card. What qualities represented by this card would you like? Is it possible that you already have, at least to some measure, those qualities?

Just as the Scarecrow and the others needed a token of their abilities to reassure them of their brain/heart/courage, you may find that you need (or at least benefit from) a token. Look at your "World of If" card again. Is there a symbol or object or shape on the card that could serve as your token? What is it? Record it.

How can you use this symbol or token as a reminder of your talents and abilities? How can you take this symbol or token as a visible and concrete reminder of both the strengths and dangers of the "World of If"? How can you use this token (which may even be the card itself) to help empower you toward achieving your goals?

Lost in the Wasteland

This exercise bears some similarities to "A Spirituality of My Own" on page 64. You may also want to refer to that exercise.

My spirituality is very important to me. I make it a high priority in my life. Throughout the years, my religious beliefs and affiliations have changed. I no longer practice the religion of my youth, but I retain many fond memories and values from that time.

I had a time in my life when I could no longer believe in one set of religious views, but I had nothing to replace those views with. As an intensely spiritual person, I was devastated, empty, and alone. I experienced severe depression, a crisis of faith, and wandered in a spiritual wilderness for several years.

Over the years, I've run into others wandering in a spiritual wilderness or wasteland. Currently, a person very dear to me is going through such an experience. I thought I would try and come up with a Tarot exercise that would be helpful, something that would have helped me during my own wasteland experience if I had been open-minded enough to try this exercise.

Choose your Tarot deck and begin your entry in your Tarot journal. Sit quietly, holding your deck in your hand or hands. Slow your breath slightly, enough to calm and center yourself, but not so much as to make yourself uncomfortable. Affirm to yourself (and any higher power to which you still feel connected) that you are earnestly and honestly seeking help and guidance from the deck of Tarot cards and from any beings, entities, powers, spirits, or levels of consciousness/levels of ego that are working in your best interests.

Think about your current state of spirituality. How do you feel? Do you feel lost? Betrayed? Empty? Scared? All of the above? Make some entries in your journal that describe your feelings. Go through your Tarot deck, faceup, looking carefully at the cards. As you see a card that seems to resonate with your spiritual state, put it aside. Which cards have you set aside? Do they seem to have anything in common? If so, what?

Looking thoughtfully at your cards, try to choose a single card that best illustrates how you feel spiritually. (You may use two or three cards if you need to, but no more than three.) Which card is this? How does it show how you feel spiritually?

Look again at your card carefully. Is there anything, anything at all on the card that could be taken as a guide, a hope, or a ray of light? Often, the hope that we need is embedded or hidden within our despair. The hope or answer is there for us, but we do not recognize it because it is not where we are looking for it. We are looking for hope or relief to come from a different place, and not the same place as our despair. No matter how hard you have to look or think, come up with something hopeful or helpful about the card of your wilderness.

What is this element of hope? Tell your journal about it.

Now, go through your deck again, faceup. This time, find from one to five cards that you feel are positive cards but that have this same element of hope on them. For instance, suppose you had chosen the 8 of Cups (*Rider Waite-Smith*) as your card of being lost. Suppose that you found the mountains in the distance to be an element of hope. Go through your deck and find from one to five cards that feel positive to you and that feature mountains on them. Tell what these cards are.

Sit quietly again, holding the cards you have chosen, both your card of despair and the other card(s) you have chosen. Affirm to yourself that you will follow the guidance of hope as a map or guide out of the wilderness.

Lay out the cards that you have chosen before you, first the wasteland card, then the other card(s). Look at them carefully.

What does your element of hope mean to you? In other words, if you have chosen mountains, what do mountains mean to you? You might want to look up your element in a dictionary or book of symbols to get additional ideas.

Draw a map of a wasteland—a body where nothing is green, where nothing grows. (I recommend doing this physically, but mentally will do.) Where are you in this wasteland? Put something there to represent you, either a stick figure or your initials or some talisman. Then, looking at your first card, draw in your element of hope, in approximately the same position that it is in on your card. Next, look at your other card(s). Where is the element of hope pictured? Draw corresponding hope on your wasteland map.

Look at the map again. It is no longer a total wasteland. There is hope. Chart a course or path toward the hope. Hope may be in more than one place. If so, choose which hope to travel to first.

Think of a concrete step you could take that would be the first step out of the wasteland. Record, date, and time that step in your journal, and then take it.

Unnamed Exercise (Grief)

I try to have a catchy and descriptive name for each of these exercises. I have a general idea of how I want the exercise to go, but the exercise itself doesn't seem to flow until I settle on a name. I struggled for over a week for a name for this exercise. No name came to me. I looked in a thesaurus, reviewed book and song titles, and reflected, but no title, and so my efforts to write the exercise were frustrated. Finally, I said to myself, "You know, grief is so painful that it goes beyond words. There seem to be no words for it. If there are no words that are adequate, no wonder you are having trouble with a name. Just call it the 'Unnamed

Exercise' or the 'Exercise Without Name.'" And so I named this exercise, the "Unnamed Exercise (Grief)," and once I did that, the exercise flowed. It flowed and flowed and flowed. It is a long exercise, with several different parts. Don't rush it.

If grief is something too basic, too central, too intrinsic, too fundamental for words, then perhaps it would be useful to use something other than words to help us deal with grief: music, dance, art, or Tarot.

There are many different kinds of loss. With any kind of loss, there seems to be a grief process that needs to be gone through, whether the loss is a death, a divorce, losing a job, having a child grow up and move away, a friendship dissolving, the loss of a dream or hope, or many other kinds of loss.

In my own life, I have experienced grief and loss. I have also sat by while others have been grief-stricken. Grief-stricken is an appropriate word, for often grief does strike us, strikes us down and pins us to the ground, much like the person in the *Rider-Waite-Smith* 10 of Swords. We are in great pain, and we are also paralyzed, lying in a pool of our own blood, watching our essence ooze out of our bodies, but incapable of doing anything, frozen, grief-struck. The Golden Dawn calls this card Lord of Ruin, and it does indeed frequently feel that way. Grief often feels like ruin, desolation, and disaster.

Grief is difficult. Loss is difficult. Many people would describe these experiences as Tower experiences, and they would not be wrong. Others feel like they are living a life of the 10 of Swords or the 9 of Swords or the 3 of Swords, and they are not wrong either. In this exercise, feel free to use any of these cards, but also feel free to use any other card in your deck.

Choose a Tarot deck and go through your deck faceup, looking at the cards. Which cards seem to picture your feelings of grief or loss? Put them aside in a small pile. Which cards are they? Narrow your choices down to three or four. You will do the rest of the exercise with these cards. If you wish, you can do the exercise with only one or two cards, but, please, no more than four.

Look at the cards carefully, one by one. If you can see the face on a card, try to mimic the expression on that face. How do you feel when your face is in that expression? Arrange your body into the same form as the form of the main character on the card. How do you feel when your body is in that position? Go through the cards in this way, one by one, and record how each facial expression and each body posture feels.

Now, go through your deck faceup again. This time I want you to look for one card that shows a character who looks like a grief survivor, someone who looks like he or she has been nailed to the ground by ten swords and yet managed to get up and walk away, someone who went through the worst that life has to offer and who lived to tell about it. Which card have you chosen? Describe this card. What makes you feel that this person is a survivor of great pain, great loss?

Look at the face and the body posture on this card. Arrange your face and body posture to match. How do you feel? Compare this feeling to the earlier experience of matching your body to the cards showing someone currently in grief. The character on this card will become your grief role model.

How do you think this person went from the first state of immense grief to his or her current state as a survivor of grief? What allowed them to move to the survivor stage? Imagine this character standing or sitting before you. Build up the image in your mind. (There are techniques to help you with this given in the exercise "Just You and Me" on page 90 if you need help.) Ask the character for advice on dealing with grief, with pain, and with loss. What does the figure say to you? Ask your role model if there is a concrete step that you could take that would help. What is that step? (Remember the difference between a concrete step and a goal or general plan of action.) Thank the person for the advice, and say goodbye.

As you deal with your loss and grief, try to hold the body posture and facial expression of your grief role model. Remember the advice. Perhaps you'll want to write it on a piece of paper to have handy, in your wallet, on your nightstand, or near your computer. Resolve to act on your concrete step as soon as possible.

Show Me the Meaning of Being Lonely

The title of this exercise is taken from a song recorded by the Backstreet Boys. The song was written by Max Martin and Herbert Crichlow. I will quote directly from the song only briefly as I don't want to violate copyright laws. You don't have to like the Backstreet Boys, pop music, or boy bands to benefit from this exercise. The title was just too appropriate to pass up as inspiration.

Some days, we long for solitude. There are days when we are ready to pull out our hair and say, "What I wouldn't give for a few hours of peace and quiet and privacy." Then there are other days when we find ourselves so lonely that loneliness seems to have grabbed our throats and squeezed, cutting off our oxygen supply and making breathing all but impossible.

I'm normally in favor of taking action to alleviate the pain of loneliness: call a friend, get out of the house, go for a walk. There are many actions that we can take to help us deal with loneliness. However, sometimes the loneliness is deeper, and it seems to seep into our bones, permeating our days and nights like an unpleasant odor that we just can't escape. According to my daughter Katherine, a big fan of the Backstreet Boys, in the video that the band filmed to go with their recording of "Show Me the Meaning of Being Lonely," references are made to their own personal lives. Brian Littrell's segment refers to his heart surgery and to his related fears. Howie Dorough's segment refers to the early death of his sister. Kevin Richardson's segment shows him watching home movies of himself playing football with his father, who died before Richardson became a member of the group. These are the kinds of loneliness that can't be alleviated by getting out of the house and doing something.

Like the lyrics of the song, these kinds of loneliness are something that we "need to walk with," that we cannot escape. Is there a purpose or lesson in this loneliness? If so, then perhaps the loneliness will stay until we learn the lesson.

Sometimes we know the lesson that we need to learn; at other times we don't. Loneliness is sometimes related to grief. If so, the grieving may take longer to deal with than dealing with the loneliness. In this exercise, let's try to identify the meaning of our current (or past) lone-liness so that we can better deal with it. This exercise may also help with grief work. If you are dealing with a grief issue, you might also want to check out the "Unnamed Exercise (Grief)" on page 74.

Choose your Tarot deck, go through the deck, faceup, and pull out any and all cards that suggest loneliness to you. These are the cards you will work with. Look at each one carefully. Do any of the charac-ters appear to be learning a lesson from their loneliness? Can you see a lesson for them to learn from loneliness (whether or not the character in the card sees it)? Put the other lonely cards (where you don't see lessons) aside.

Name the cards where you can see lessons, and record them and what those lessons are, in your opinion, in your Tarot journal. Choose one of these cards to work with further. You can choose one faceup because you want to work with it further, or you can turn them over, rearrange, and randomly choose one.

You are now going to do some imaginary role-playing. Imagine that the lonely person in the card is a friend of yours. Name a real-life friend or make up a name. This friend has a lesson to learn from lone-liness, and although he or she is striving hard, your friend is just not quite "getting it." (Perhaps he or she needs to try the "Jump-Start" exercise on page 36. Perhaps he or she needs a little help.)

Except for the one card that you are working with, put all of the rest of the cards back with your deck. Go through your deck faceup again. This time look for a wise person to help your friend. Sometimes we need tough wise people, and sometimes we need gentle wise people. Which kind does your friend need? Which card have you cho-sen to be the wise person for your friend? Why?

Imagine the wise person standing before your friend with love and compassion, but also with firmness and absolute honesty. What would the wise person say? Record this conversation in your journal. In your opinion, is this what your friend needs to hear? Can you value and trust the word of the wise person? If not, then this exercise is at an end.

If so, then you sit down before this wise person and ask for guid-ance in finding the meaning of your loneliness. What does the wise one tell you? Is the advice the same or different from what the wise person told your friend?

Think of a concrete step that you can do within the next few days that will start you on the way to learning from your lesson of loneliness. Share the step with your journal. Commit to taking that step.

Healing Sun

This exercise can be used as a general healing exercise for your current self, or it can be applied to a particular health issue. Please decide in advance which way you are going to use it before you proceed.

Choose a Tarot deck and record the name of the deck. Go through your deck and pull out the Sun card. Many cards can be useful for healing work, but in this exercise you will use the Sun card as your first healing card.

Using the Golden Dawn system of correspondences (see Appendices B and C), the Sun card corresponds to the Sun. The Sun manifests in our lives in many different ways. The wintry Sun of Capricorn is different from the fiery Sun of Leo. The eager Sun of Aries is different from the meditative Sun of Pisces. The Sun is a wonderful energy for healing: warm, vital, life-giving, but how it works best in your own life will probably depend on your sign of the zodiac.

What sign are you? Choosing from the list in Appendix B (or making appropriate changes if you already use a different set of correspondences), find the card that represents your Sun sign.

You will now have two cards: the Sun and a card corresponding to the sign that the Sun was in when you were born. Study the two cards side by side. What message do they give you? Can you apply any of this message to your overall health or to a current health issue?

Leaving these two cards out of the deck, shuffle the rest of your deck. Randomly choose one more card to represent the advice of the Tarot for a means, a method, or a message to you about your health in the area that you have previously chosen (overall for this time of life or a particular issue). What is the card? Does it have anything in common with either of your other two cards? If so, what?

Here is a list of parts of the body associated with various cards, based on astrology and the Golden Dawn correspondences.

Emperor = head

Hierophant = throat and lower jaw

Lovers = lungs and arms

Chariot = breast and stomach

Strength = heart

Hermit = intestines and liver

Justice = kidneys and lower back

Death = genitals, bladder, and rectum

Temperance = hips and thighs

Devil = knees and lower legs

Star = ankles

Moon = feet

Go to a quiet place where you can lie down. You might want to put on some meditation music or light a candle or incense. Lie down with your three Tarot cards in your hand. Place the Sun card over your heart. Place your card representing your Sun sign on the part of the body associated with that sign. Place the third card on the area where you have a specific concern. If you are doing this exercise about your overall health for your time of life and not a specific concern, put the third card on your solar plexus, the third chakra which is at your diaphragm.

At this point you are lying down with three cards on your body: the Sun card on your heart, your Sun sign card on the area of your body ruled by that sign, and the third card on either your solar plexus or a part of your body representing your health concern.

Be very still. Breathe slowly. Count your heartbeats. When you have counted sixty heartbeats, roll to your side. Put the three cards before you, in the order that they were positioned on your body. Study them again, still lying on your side, still breathing slowly.

Not addressing the cards themselves but rather addressing the energies represented by the cards (this distinction is important), ask the Sun's energy to bless you through the positive expression of your Sun sign card.

You can think of the Sun as an aspect of the Divine, as a manifestation of Divinity, as an expression of the Divine, as an aspect of your subconscious, as your higher self. Use whatever way of thinking about the Sun works best with your personal spirituality and philosophy.

Ask the Sun's energy to send you a message via the third card. You may have already received this message in your earlier study and quiet time. If not, be still and wait for a message. When you receive it, thank the energy of the Sun for sending you these messages.

Using all three cards, but focusing especially on the third card, what concrete step can you take to help you with improving your health and your attitude toward your health?

Time/Space Experiment

This exercise is different from most of the other exercises. First, it has no clear direction or focus. There is no desired answer or objective. The only purpose to this exercise is to do it honestly and to observe what happens. The second difference is that this exercise will take several days to perform and will require more than one Tarot deck. To do this exercise, you'll need at least three cards drawn over three days— each from a different deck, and you may use seven cards drawn over seven days—each from a different deck. If you skip a day, that's okay. Just use the next day. If you skip two days, please start over or just use the days that you have if you've already gotten three days.

The concept of this experimental exercise is related to quantum physics, or at least to my extremely challenged understanding of it. From what I know, Newtonian physics works just fine as long as we are plugging along at *normal* speeds. However, as we approach (and surpass) the speed of light, laws of Newtonian physics are replaced by other laws, which are called quantum physics. Taking this as inspiration, you are going to try working with your cards at two sets of speeds, to see what the results of different speeds have on your perception of the Tarot and on the impressions/discoveries that you gain from the Tarot.

This exercise requires that you use three to seven different Tarot decks. If you do not have at least three different Tarot decks, there are inventive workarounds possible, but I do not recommend that you do this exercise unless you have access to several different decks. Without multiple decks, the exercise just gets too complex.

Day One: Choose a Tarot deck. Record the name of the deck in your journal. Hold the deck in your hands, thinking, "What truth do I most need to realize in my life at the present time?" In whatever manner you prefer, choose a card. Don't look at the card at this time. Put it away, separate from the rest of your cards.

Day Two: Choose a Tarot deck. It should be a different deck from the deck that you used on Day One because that deck currently is missing one card, and you want to use a complete deck for this exercise. Record the name of the deck. Hold the deck in your hands, thinking, "What truth do I most need to realize in my life at the present time?" In whatever manner you prefer, choose a card. Don't look at the card at this time. Put it away, separate from the rest of your cards. Do not attempt to meditate or work with or study the card at this time.

Days Three to Seven: Choose a Tarot deck. It should be a different deck for each day and different from the decks used for the first two days. Record the name of the deck. Hold the deck in your hands, thinking, "What truth do I most need to realize in my life at the present time?" In whatever manner you prefer, choose a card. Don't look at the card at this time. Put it away, separate from the rest of your cards. Do not attempt to meditate or work with or study the card at this time. Continue in the same vein for as many days as you want to work the exercise. You may stop the experiment after three days, or you may continue it for seven days.

Without looking (or with looking only as little as possible) assemble your three to seven cards, facedown in a pile in the order in which they were drawn.

If you like to make preparations for meditation, do so before continuing. You may light incense and a candle, or ring a gong, or turn the ringer off the telephone. Whatever you do to help yourself enter a contemplative stage, please do so now.

Without looking at them, gather your cards for this exercise in their chronological order. Ask, "What truth do I most need to realize in my life at the present time?" Then, as quickly as you can, flip through the cards, faceup, looking at each one for only a second or a fraction of a second. Go through the cards over and over, as fast as you can. Don't stop to consciously think, but allow the images to impress themselves on your subconscious mind. When you have a single image or idea or word or thought that seems to come to you, stop. Write down that image or idea or thought.

Next, lay out the cards before you in a circle or other closed shape (triangle, square, pentagon). The shape will vary depending on how many cards you use. Slowly, thoughtfully, deliberately, study the cards. Look at the cards and ask, "What truth do I most need to realize in my life at the present time?" Looking at the cards as a group, in their closed layout, what ideas, words, or thoughts come to you? Write them down. Don't break the layout down into individual cards. Try to see the overall pattern, the overall theme, the overall impact of the cards.

Finally, take each card and make it your *card for the day*, meditating on the card, taking it for your theme card for the day, your meditation for the day. This will take three to seven days to perform, depending on how many cards you initially chose. What lessons do you learn from each card, after carrying it with you for an entire day?

You have now looked at the same three to seven cards in three different ways—moving very quickly in sequence, being still but looked at as a single unit, and each card as a theme card for a twenty-four-hour period. What have you learned different from each way? How has the message been the same? How has it been different? Did one method resonate more for you than the others? What is the truth that you most need to realize at the present time?

If you have a Tarot buddy, have your friend also do this exercise and compare notes. You will be very surprised to see how your friend's experience will be different from your own. No concrete step for this exercise.

What Tarot Is to Me

As a Tarot teacher, I'm often asked, "What is Tarot to you?" and, "How has Tarot changed your life?" In several web-page articles, I have written answers that are all accurate and all incomplete. However, no matter how extensively I've written about the subject, there is actually no way to fully answer the question without using Tarot itself as a medium.

Therefore, I've devised a simple exercise to help describe what Tarot is to me. I believe that many of you can use it to help you explain what Tarot is to you as well. Anyone who has studied Tarot for any time at all is going to get asked, "Why Tarot? What do you get from it? Why would you want to study that?" This exercise can be adapted to help explain anything you love that others have a hard time understanding—runes, goddess study, Reiki, astrology, and more.

Choose your Tarot deck and record it in your journal. Think about the questions, "What does Tarot mean to me on a physical or material level? What gifts does Tarot bring to me on this plane?" Go through your deck faceup, and choose one card that best answers your questions. What is that card?

Think about the questions, "What does Tarot mean to me on an intellectual or mental level? What gifts does Tarot bring to me on this plane?" Go through your deck faceup, and choose one card that best answers your questions. What is that card?

Think about the questions, "What does Tarot mean to me on an emotional or social level? What gifts does Tarot bring to me on this plane?" Go through your deck faceup, and choose one card that best answers your questions. What is that card?

Think about the questions, "What does Tarot mean to me on a spiritual level? What gifts does Tarot bring to me on this plane?" Go through your deck faceup, and choose one card that best answers your questions. What is that card?

At this point, you should have four cards in front of you. Do your best to have only four cards (I know that some of you have difficulty narrowing down your choices).

You now have a choice. You can either record the cards that you've chosen and put them back in your deck, or you can use a second Tarot deck. If you are using a second deck, be sure to record the name of that deck in your journal alongside the name of the first deck. The point is that for this second part of the exercise, you want to have all seventy-eight cards available to come up.

Shuffle your deck. Ask your Tarot deck to show you what it brings to you physically, mentally, emotionally, and spiritually. In whatever fashion that you normally choose cards without looking (off the top of the deck, from the deck fanned out in front of you, or another method), choose a card for each group of questions (without looking at the faces). You will have four new cards, randomly chosen.

What are the four cards? Discuss the similarities and differences between the first set of four cards and the second set of four cards. What have you learned about your relationship with the Tarot from looking at this second set of cards? Where there any surprises? If so, what? Which set of cards do you prefer, the ones you chose deliberately or the ones you chose randomly? Which set seems more accurate?

Now, going through either of your decks (if you used two) faceup, choose one card to represent what you wish your relationship with Tarot was like. What is this card? How does it describe what you wish your relationship with Tarot was like?

Decide to begin working toward that relationship today. Choose one concrete step to represent this beginning. What is that concrete step?

FOUR

EXERCISES FOR SPECIAL OCCASIONS AND SITUATIONS

These exercises are sometimes easy, sometimes fun, sometimes complex. Some of them might be considered easy, and some of them are very difficult. I've put them in a separate chapter because, more than anything, they do seem designed for special situations and occasions, whereas the exercises in the other chapters seem more general purpose exercises that can be done at any time and aren't targeted for special occasions. The theme of relationship and romance seems to show up in several of these exercises.

My Mother, My Self

Go through your deck faceup and choose a card that best represents your mother to you. How do you feel about this card? How is this card like your mother? How is this card unlike your mother? How does this card illustrate your feelings toward your mother? Would you prefer that your mother were more like a different card? If so, why? If so, which card?

Now, go through your deck faceup again. Choose a card to illustrate how you *mother* (nurture) yourself—or in the case of some of us, don't nurture yourself. This is not a card to describe what kind of mother you are to other people. This is a card to illustrate how you take care of yourself, how you nurture yourself, how you do for yourself those things that have traditionally been done for others by mothers. Is this how you want to mother yourself? What does this say to you about how you treat yourself? What card would you prefer for how you mother yourself?

What is the relationship between how you see your mother and how you mother yourself, based on the cards that you have chosen? How do you feel about this relationship? Devise a concrete step that you can take in the next twenty-four hours to nurture yourself. Depending on your needs, you may need to be prodded into making changes in your life. You may need a long bubble bath. You may need a good meal cooked by someone else, even if it is a cook at a restaurant or the neighborhood deli. You may need to hire a maid for a day. Whatever would be the best way to nurture yourself in the here and now, do it.

My Father's Eyes

I long wanted to write a companion exercise for "My Mother, My Self," an exercise that dealt with issues with our fathers. However, I didn't want it to be a copycat exercise, an exercise where I just went through and substituted a few words, turning "mother" into "father" and "nurturing" into "respect." One day, the title of Eric Clapton's song, "My Father's Eyes" just kept running through my mind—not the song itself, but the title, which was rather strange. After several hours of this, I began to pay attention, and then it hit me, "Aha! Now I have the hook for a father exercise!"

According to one tradition, the Emperor is the father figure in the Tarot deck; he is the universal father. Also, according to this tradition, the Hebrew letter associated with the Emperor is *Heh*, which means "window." The quality of sight is also attributed to the Emperor, so the song title "My Father's Eyes" has a built-in connection to the Emperor card.

This exercise was designed to facilitate an epiphany and/or healing moment in your relationship with your father or a father figure in your life. This exercise may prove helpful even if your father has already passed on.

For the purposes of this exercise, we are going to use the Emperor card as the Universal Father of the Tarot deck. Choose a Tarot deck and pull out the Emperor. Study the picture. In particular, study the eyes of the Emperor.

Next, go through your deck and look for a card whose eyes seem to match your father's eyes. This can be any card in the deck. You are not so much looking for a father figure card as a card whose eyes match *your* father's eyes. What card did you choose? How do the eyes of this card resemble the eyes of your father? Does the picture on this card resemble your father in any other way?

Does the meaning of this card reveal anything about your father? If so, what?

Hold the Emperor card and the card that you have chosen so that they face one another, so that the figures in the cards are looking at each other, eye-to-eye. If the Universal Father were to speak to your father, what would he say? What words of wisdom, encouragement, and comfort would he give?

Would he also take your father to task for failures or weaknesses? If so, how would he sternly but fairly speak to your father about these failures and weaknesses?

Now, go through your deck and choose a second card faceup. This card is to represent how you feel about yourself in your relationship with your father. It can be the card that you normally use to represent yourself, but it will probably be a different card. What mode or personality do you slip into when you are with your father? Use a card that shows you as you feel about yourself as a son or daughter to your father.

Put the Emperor card aside. Take the card representing your father and the card representing yourself and face them together. Imagine your father, full of the message of the Universal Father, speaking to you. This is the message that your father's higher self would give to your higher self. This is the message that your father's higher self has always wanted to give to you but, for one reason or another, has never been able to share with you. What does your father say?

Listen. How does this message make you feel? How is this message different from the normal messages that your father has given you? How is this message similar to other messages that your father has given you?

Take the rest of your deck and shuffle it. You are going to ask the Tarot to share with you an insight, a message to you about your father and your relationship with him. In whatever manner you normally choose an unseen card, choose a card. What is it? What does this tell you about your father and your relationship with him? What action might you take based on this card? How will the message of this card help you to go ahead in your personal growth?

You may wish to set the four cards of this exercise aside for the next few days so that you can continue to see them and meditate on their messages to you. Seeing them will also encourage you to take your concrete action based on the message that you received.

Just You and Me

As I was thinking of how to title this exercise, the old Chicago song came to mind, "Just you and me, simple and free." Often we long for relationships to be simple and free, but, in actuality, relationships are rarely, if ever, simple and free. If a relationship isn't simple or free, what is it? It can be many things, and if it is a long-term relationship, it *will* be many things as relationships are never static, always changing.

This exercise is written as a look at a current relationship, but you could also adapt it for past relationships, and possibly for future ones as well. It is appropriate for any kind of relationship: romantic, parent/child, siblings, friends, boss/employee, coworkers, or others. This exercise is written for two people in a relationship, but it could also be adapted for three to four persons when there is a small group dynamic that you wish to examine. There are two parts: an analytical part and an imaginative part. Some of you will find one part hard and the other part easy.

Think of a relationship that you would like to explore. It could be one that is currently causing you some trouble or distress, or one about which you would simply like a little more understanding. Name the relationship in your journal, using either the person's name or choosing a title or pseudonym (Boss, Mom, Daughter, "Cissy," "Junior," "Bubba," whatever). Choose your Tarot deck and record it in your journal as well.

Go through your deck, faceup. Choose a card that you feel most closely represents you. (It doesn't need to be a court card or even to agree with you in gender or age.) Record the name of the card. How does this card depict you? How does it differ? Choose a card that you feel most closely represents the other person. Record the name of the card. How does this card depict the other person? How does it differ?

Now, look at the two cards together. Do they face each other or away? Do they both face right or both face left? What are the colors like in each card? Look at the faces of each character. Look at the symbols. Look at the gestures and posture. How do you think that these two cards will get along? What will be their obvious compatibilities? What will be their obvious differences? What does this tell you about a potential or real relationship between the people in these cards? What does this tell you about your relationship with the other person? Do you have any additional insights about your relationship from studying these cards together?

At this point, you may wish to turn off the ringer on your phone and put aside any distractions. You will want a few minutes of quiet, uninterrupted time. Look at the card you have chosen to represent you. See if you can visualize yourself as that card.

There are several techniques for this kind of work, which is often called creative visualization. Some people can do this easily, and others have more trouble with it. If you can't visualize this, then try to just imagine "what if," or try to use your other senses, such as hearing or touch, rather than seeing. The experience will be more vivid if you use several different senses. If you have trouble with this part, don't push it, just play "pretend" instead. You can get a great deal of information from creative visualization even if you don't *see* things. Just use your other senses and/or your imagination and don't get hung up on the visualization part of the term "creative visualization."

See if you can be the Queen of Swords on top of the windy hill, or see if you can be the woman in the 9 of Pentacles in her cozy garden or whatever card you have chosen. Are you there? Once you successfully can visualize (or imagine) yourself in the setting of your card, then expand your horizons, your line of vision, until you can "see" the person in the other card. Where is the person? What is he or she doing? How far away is the figure?

You wish to talk to the other person. Does he or she approach you or do you do the approaching? What is the expression on your face now? How do you feel? What is the expression on the other person's face? What do you do? What does the other person do? Do either of you speak? If so, what do you say? Do you exchange gestures or tokens? If so, what?

Let this conversation flow naturally. Observe the details of what happens, but do not try to orchestrate it or make things happen. After a while, the interchange is over. One or both of you turn and walk away. How do you feel? Have you come to any understanding? What have you learned?

Allow your focus to slide out of the card so that you are once again yourself in the present. It may be helpful to turn the cards over, face-down, to symbolically show that you are now anchored in this reality. Share any additional thoughts that you have received from either part of this exercise.

Is there a concrete step you could take to improve your relationship or to resolve it or to end it, if necessary? Share this step with your journal.

Dream Lover

This exercise is good if you are not in a relationship, if you are in a troubled relationship, or if you are in a good relationship. The only people who might not be interested in it are those who are not in a relationship, have never been in a relationship, and who have no desire to ever be in a relationship. There is nothing wrong with them, but they are in the minority.

Choose your deck and go through it slowly, faceup. Choose a card that seems to you to most closely represent your ideal or dream lover. The gender of the card does not matter. If you are normally attracted to men, feel free to chose a card with a woman on it if the woman represents the qualities that you most desire.

What do you like about this card? What makes it attractive to you? What kind of lover do you think the embodiment of this card would be like?

Now, go through the deck again. This time choose a card for you—as you are now, this very moment. Why is this card like you? How do you feel about this card? Are you happy with this choice or unhappy?

Look at the two cards together. What kind of relationship do you think the two cards will have? Why? What does this tell you about yourself? What does this tell you about your concept of an ideal lover? How realistic are your expectations?

For example, did you choose the Knight of Wands for your dream lover and the High Priestess for yourself? How would these two cards get along? What strengths and weaknesses would they have as a couple?

How closely is the dream lover card related to the people in your present and past relationships? What does this tell you about the relationships that you have been in or may currently be in? What goals can you set for present and future relationships, based on your discoveries? What step can you take today toward achieving those goals?

Difficult Relationships

This is an exercise written in response to a request. The request was for an exercise for dealing with stepchildren and/or ex-spouses, but I felt that in-laws and other difficult relationships could be included, so I've tried to make the exercise general and flexible enough to apply to all difficult relationships. In addition, I would recommend the exercises "My Mother, My Self," "Just You and Me," and "Healing Heart" for help with difficult relationships.

Although many of these exercises make references to music, this exercise makes direct use of music. Music is indeed healing, and this exercise freely makes use of the healing qualities of music. Get out your boom box and your CDs and get ready to have some fun as you explore a difficult relationship.

Choose a particular difficult relationship. Choose your Tarot deck. Record both in your Tarot journal. Go through your deck, faceup, and choose a card for yourself in the relationship (which may be different from the card that you normally think of for yourself or it may be the same), and choose a card for the other person. What are the cards? Why did you choose them?

Next, choose a song to represent the relationship. This may be something like "Crazy" if the other person drives you crazy, or "All Shook Up" if the other person drives you to shaking like a leaf, or "Fly" if you just want to fly away and forget that the other person exists. What song did you choose? Why?

Next, get out your two cards, one for you and one for the other person. Put on a recording of the song if you have it (if you don't, hum, or play the song in your head). Let your cards dance the song, just like you would dance puppets. How does each card dance? What do you see?

Next, you dance as yourself in the relationship. How do you feel? Do you dance the same way that you had the card representing you dance? If not, how is it different?

Then, dance as the other person in the relationship. How do you feel? Do you dance the same way as you had the card representing the other person dancing? If not, how is it different? What did you learn by dancing as the other person? Was it strange to dance as someone else? Did you have any insights into the other person's actions, thoughts, or motivations?

Put your two cards back in the deck and shuffle it. With the music still playing (you may have to play it over several times during this exercise), ask, "What is the best possible outcome of this relationship?" Choose a card, facedown. Turn it over. What is the card? How do you interpret it?

Even if the card is usually considered negative, do not interpret it totally negatively because the best possible outcome will have some positive features. For example, if you get the Tower card, one possible interpretation would be that the relationship needs to start over from the ground up—a fresh start. In a case like this, I would not interpret the Tower as saying that the best possible outcome for the relationship would be to end it, although, for some relationships, that may eventually be the case.

Think of a song that represents this best possible outcome for you. What is the name of the song? Do you own a copy of it? If so, listen to it at this time.

After you have chosen the card for the best possible outcome and interpreted it, choose a second card, facedown. Ask, "What can I do to improve this relationship?" Turn the card over. What is it? What is a concrete step that you can take to help improve the relationship?

For the next few days, if you have trouble with the relationship, pull out the cards that you've used for this exercise—the card for you, for the other person, for the best possible outcome, and what you can do to help. Put the cards before you. Listen to the music that represents the best possible outcome while you meditate on the cards.

Wedding

Weddings are powerful spiritual and symbolic occasions, even the simplest weddings, the most ornate ones, legal weddings, or ones without legal stamps of approval. There is great power present for the bride and groom (or bride and bride, or groom and groom), for those officiating, and for all of those present. Even watching a videotape of a wedding can bring up deep emotions. This exercise may touch some sensitive spots, perhaps some surprising spots.

Some of us are in happy marriages. Some of us are in unhappy marriages. Some of us want to be married; others are happily unmarried. Some of us may have recently lost a marriage partner. No matter what our marital status, weddings are still powerful. In this Tarot exercise, I want to draw upon the power of weddings.

Tell your Tarot journal which Tarot deck you are using. Go through your deck, faceup. Choose a card that most represents weddings to you. Record the card and why this card seems to represent weddings to you. I am not talking about a card that reflects marriage, but weddings. There is a difference.

Have you ever attended a wedding that seemed reflected in this card? If so, tell about it. If not, imagine a wedding that, to you, would reflect this card, and tell about your imagined wedding ceremony.

In the wedding ceremony that you have described, who are you? Are you the bride or groom? Are you the minister or officiant? Are you the maid of honor or best man? Are you a parent of the bride or groom? Are you an honored guest? Are you the photographer or the caterer? Your answer here is spiritual or symbolic rather than real. In other words, if you have a daughter soon to be married, you could still be the bride or groom and not the mother or father of the bride or groom.

Look again at the Tarot card you have chosen. Put yourself in the card. If you are the caterer, and there is no caterer in the card, put yourself mentally in the card anyway. Describe your wedding role as inspired by your Tarot card. How does this differ (or not differ) from how you normally see yourself? Would you like to see yourself as more or less like the role inspired by your card? Choose a concrete step that will indicate a willingness to become more like your wedding self. Record that concrete step.

This concrete step is probably the one single most important part of the exercise.

Healing Hands

There are numerous ways to use Tarot for healing—many Tarot cards give a message of healing. This exercise looks at the hands of healing. You can do it as an intellectual exercise now, or, if you are in need of healing, this exercise may have more immediate application.

Often, when we think of healing, we think of the hands. Ancient Christians prayed and laid hands on people to heal them. Reiki practitioners heal by using their hands. Massage therapists heal by touch, as do foot reflexologists and many others. The hands are strong tools for healing.

Look through your deck faceup. Most of you are going to choose two cards. Some of you may find one card that will serve a dual purpose. First, look for a card that seems to represent a healer to you, someone whom you feel would be a good personal healer, not necessarily a card that represents a global or worldwide healer. Which card is it? Why does it suggest healer to you? What about this card makes you want the figure on it for your personal healer?

Second, look for a card with hand placements or gestures that look like they are going to touch you in a loving and healing manner. In other words, look specifically at hands when you are looking for this second card. Which hands seem to you to be hands of healing, hands that have the healing touch? What is it about the body language on this card that speaks to you? Describe the gesture. You may choose the same card as the first one for this, or you may choose a second card.

Picture your healing card in your mind. Third, picture the hands from the second card. Can you visualize or imagine this? (You may want to consult the "Just You and Me" exercise on page 90 for suggestions on creative visualization.) Once you have this picture or concept in mind, then put yourself into the picture. You are going to ask the figure from the first card to touch you with the healing hands of the second card.

If you have trouble with this exercise, that's fine. Some people take to creative visualization very easily and others do not. If you have trouble, try this alternate version. Do the exercise as stated until you get to the part about, "Picture your healing card. . . ." At that point, ask yourself, "What if the figure from the first card used the gestures of the second card and touched me? What would happen?"

In other words, how would you feel if the figure in the first card touched you with the hands of the second card? What effect would the gestures or touch of the second card have upon you if the main character of the first card did them to or toward you? Use your imagination to come up with an answer and record that.

In either case, what happens? How do you feel about what happens? No concrete step for this exercise.

Healing Heart: An Exercise for Emotional Wounds

This exercise is different from some of the others and uses art therapy. It can be done alone or with friends. I like doing it in a group myself. No previous Tarot experience is necessary.

You'll need several things for this exercise. Go ahead and assemble your materials before beginning the exercise because once you start, you'll want to finish it all in one sitting, if possible.

Supplies needed:

3 of Swords card showing a heart pierced by three swords—not necessarily from the *Rider-Waite-Smith* deck, just any deck that shows this sort of image

3 toothpicks, or 3 cocktail spears or kabob skewers, per person

2 sheets of stiff red paper per person (can be construction paper)

1 sheet of stiff green or gold paper per person

Assorted sheets of colored paper or tissue paper (optional, and does not need to be stiff)

Glue

Scissors

Markers, pens, crayons, and/or washable paints

Any other art supplies that you like to use and have on hand

Burning candle

Fire-safe dish or tray or bowl

Photograph of yourself when you were feeling healthy and happy and whole

Burning incense (optional)

Light your candle and incense. Look at the flame. Smell the incense. Ask your Spiritual Source to aid you in a healing exercise.

Look at the 3 of Swords. Does this in any way resemble how your heart feels?

Take a sheet of the red paper. Cut it into the shape of a heart. Take the toothpicks or cocktail spears or kabob skewers and pierce your paper heart so that it looks like the 3 of Swords. Using scissors and other tools and materials, create a physical heart that looks like your heart feels. Describe what this heart looks like and feels like.

Without going into the specifics of your situation, and concentrating on your feelings only (not who did what or said what to whom), tell your Tarot journal about your wounded heart. A typical response might be, "My heart feels squeezed and dried out, withered like a prune, and stomped flat by a steam roller." Do not assign blame to anyone or anything. You are describing your feelings and how your heart looks, based on your feelings. After you have done this, put your wounded paper heart aside.

Now, look at the photograph of yourself when you were feeling healthy and happy and whole. Describe how your heart felt then. Again, don't go into the specifics of the situation; concentrate on your feelings.

Taking the other sheet of red paper, make another paper heart. Decorate this one so that it resembles how your healthy, happy heart felt. Describe this heart.

You can transform your current wounded heart into your healthy heart. This transformation will probably not be instantaneous—although it could be. The first step in this transformation is letting go of your wounded heart. To represent that you are letting go of your wounded heart, lift it to the candle and let it catch fire. Drop the burning heart into the fire-safe container.

Take the healthy paper heart and hold it over the incense, then put it over your chest where your physical heart is. Invite the healing represented by the healthy paper heart to transform your wounded heart into a healed heart. Spend several seconds or several minutes of meditation at this point, if you wish.

When you are done, cut a large square of the green or gold paper. This square is to be a background for your healthy heart, a frame for it. Green and gold are considered healing colors in different traditions, and either color will do. By mounting your heart on a healing background, you are making the paper heart a more powerful physical symbol for healing.

Think of a concrete step or action that you could take in your life to represent your choice to go toward healing. What is this step? Record it in your journal.

Put your healthy paper heart in a prominent place—by your bed, on a mirror, at your computer—a place where you will see it often. Every time you see it, remind yourself of how your heart felt when it was healthy. Invite your heart to experience those feelings again and again.

You might like to use the "Love Break" and "Healing Hands" exercises to help as a follow-up to this exercise. Here's to healthy, happy, whole hearts for all of us.

Distant Prayers

Many times in life, we will feel the urge to send distant prayers. Even people who don't believe in prayer often feel the urge to send light, energy, hope, thoughts, whatever. There are many times when such a need is evident: a friend or relative who is ill, a national crisis, a regional catastrophe. Here is an exercise that uses Tarot as a focus for distant prayers.

Have a particular person or situation in mind about which you feel helpless, but that you wish there was something you could do to help. Choose your deck and go through the deck faceup, looking for a card that seems to best depict the situation.

Look at the card. Tell your journal how this card depicts the situation that you have in mind. Be sure to give details of the card and to relate those to specific details of the situation.

Now, go through your deck faceup again. This time, choose the card that to you would represent the best possible outcome. Describe this card and relate how, in your mind, this would be the best possible outcome.

Finally, go through your deck a third time. This time, choose a deck that, to you, represents complete surrender to a great good or a great

holiness or a great light or a divine purpose. Tell how the card you
chose resembles this concept.

Lay all three cards out before you, left to right. First, imagine the
situation in your mind, as represented by the Tarot card. Second,
address whatever power, being, state of mind, higher self, or whatever
you turn to when you are sending out pleas and thoughts for hope
and guidance. Say, "_____ (form of address comfortable to you), I
lift up this situation. My hope for this situation is _____ (depicted
by Card #2). However, I surrender this situation to you (image of
Card #3), and ask for personal peace and direction in this matter."

Let me interject a note of explanation. As my students began working through this exercise, it became clear that people were not understanding the purpose of Card #3. Card #3 is not what you are praying
for or hoping for—that is almost exactly what Card #2 is. Card #3 is
the archetype, energy, deity, whatever, to which you surrender the situation. Card #3 does not represent an outcome or hope or wish or
prayer. It represents the being to which you address your hope or wish
or prayer.

For example, if you are a traditional Christian, you might pick a
card that reminds you of Jesus or of God the Father. If you are a Goddess worshipper, you might pick a card that represents your particular
Goddess or the face of the Goddess you prefer. If you are Buddhist,
which card reminds you of Buddha? If you pray to angels or saints or
spirits, which card looks most like your favorite angel or saint or spirit? If you don't pray to any being but instead draw on a Higher Power
of indefinite origins, which card reminds you of this Higher Power? If
you direct prayers and hopes to your own higher self, which card most
represents your higher self?

I'm not talking about praying to a card but about using a card to
represent to whom/what you pray (hope, mediate, direct energy,
whatever) so that you can have a visual focus.

As a further note, let me interject that I don't recommend praying
for others without their permission except in the general way of sending white light or asking Deity for the greatest good in a situation. We
don't always know what the greatest good is because of our limited

wisdom and understanding, and so I do not presume to dictate to the Universe what actions should be taken. It is with this belief that I wrote this exercise, not requesting a specific action, but, instead, expressing the wish of the person working the exercise and surrendering the situation to the hands of Divine Providence that, because of greater wisdom and understanding, does know the greatest good for all situations. Several people who have worked this exercise have had trouble with this concept and continue to want to give orders to Divinity on what should be done in a situation. That is not what this exercise is about.

When you finish the exercise, you may or may not have an instant sense of peace or direction. If you do, please record it in your journal. Sometimes this peace or direction comes later. By direction, I mean something that you personally could do to aid the situation, either symbolically or practically. A symbolic action would be to light a candle. A practical action would be to send money or go in person to offer aid. There are many other symbolic and practical actions, of course, and they will vary depending on the circumstance.

Prosperity and Abundance

This exercise was adapted from a technique that I learned from Mary Greer called "Look at a Card." It is one of the most popular of the exercises that I've written. I don't know if it is because of the exercise itself or because prosperity and abundance are issues that so many people are preoccupied with.

Go through your deck, faceup, and choose a card that seems to you to represent prosperity, wealth, abundance, or plenty. You may choose to limit your search to just the Major Arcana or just the Pentacles, or to the Majors and the Pentacles. You may use the whole deck.

Name your deck and name your card in your Tarot journal. Look at the card. Describe briefly what you see on the card—images, symbols, objects. Look at the card again. Describe briefly how you feel when you look at the card. Do not try to read or interpret the card.

Look at the card again. What about the card specifically makes you think of plenty, prosperity, abundance, and wealth? Is there something unspecific about the card that also makes you think or feel this way? Some subtle impression of some kind of wealth? If so, what is it?

Make up a brief story about the card, something that could humorously appear in any financial periodical. For example, for the 3 of Wands in the *Robin Wood* deck, you could say, "Entrepreneur expands fleet, sends out new ships to the Far East. Expected yield is risky but if he pulls it off, he'll quadruple his net wealth. When interviewed, Lord Flame said, 'I felt that the timing was right, felt that I had to follow my dream, had to act upon my instincts. In the past, I've prospered by listening to my inner voice, so I'm not going to stop now.'"

Retell the story, only this time, with yourself as the central person in the story. Read the second version of the story carefully. What message does it give you about your attitudes toward prosperity? What ideas does it give you about improving your prosperity?

How can you improve your prosperity by using your Tarot card as a role model? Think of a concrete step that you can take within the next forty-eight hours, using your prosperity and abundance Tarot model. Record this step and resolve to do it.

Bone Weary/Soul Weary

We've all had days or weeks or months when we've felt not just tired, but bone weary, soul weary. We wonder how much longer we can keep going without crashing—physically, mentally, emotionally, or spiritually, or some combination of these. In fact, we wonder (and others wonder too), "How am I still standing?"

I can almost hear you saying, "Ah, yes! I've been there." I hope you aren't there right now. Still, we've had those days, and we'll probably have them again.

Think of a time when you felt bone weary or soul weary. Go through your Tarot deck, faceup. Choose a card that depicts how you feel when you are bone weary or soul weary. Tell your Tarot journal the name of the card. Tell how the card fits your feelings. Tell how the card does not fit your feelings.

Now, think back to that same specific bone-weary/soul-weary time. If you could have had some one thing as a help or an aid, what would it have been? Go through your Tarot deck faceup again. Do you see a card that represents some one thing that you would have liked as a help or an aid? Which card is it? How do you see it as a help or aid? Does it fall short in any way of what you wanted or needed? If so, how?

Now, sit quietly for a moment. How might you use the energy or skills or presence of this second Tarot card to avoid getting bone weary or soul weary in the future? Think of a concrete step that you could take the next time you start to get tired that would help you avoid the overwhelming bone-weary/soul-weary tiredness. What is that step? Choose a Tarot card to represent that step.

Driving My Car

At one time, we had a series of fender-benders in my household. My older daughter, Mary Frances, had three in less than two months; I had one; and my younger daughter, Katherine, who had only a learner's permit at the time, also had an accident while taking a practice drive with her father. From these real-life incidents, it seemed as if a car or driving exercise would be worthwhile.

Certainly, there are enough songs about cars: "Little Deuce Coupe," "Pink Cadillac," "Little Red Corvette," and so on. Okay, so not all of them are really about cars and driving, but in our society, cars and driving are motifs or symbols of other issues. Do this exercise on a straightforward level about cars and driving, or do it on a deeper level and find out what cars and driving represent for you.

Choose your Tarot deck and go through your deck faceup. Choose a card that has the same essence, feel, mood, or image as that of your ideal car (not necessarily the car that you are currently driving). How does this card describe or depict your ideal car?

Now, go through your deck again. This time choose a card that seems to best reflect your attitudes and skills toward driving. What card is it? How does it reflect your attitudes and skills?

Go through your deck a third time. This time choose a card that seems to reflect your concept of an ideal driver—the kind of driver that you would like to be and also the kind of driver that you would like the other people on the road to be. What card is it? How does this reflect your concept of an ideal driver?

Compare your three cards. How are they similar? How are they different? What insights do you have about your ideals for cars and driving versus the reality of your current driving skills and attitudes? How can you move more toward your ideal?

Give a concrete step you can take that will move you closer to your ideal as a driver.

It's a Holiday

Choose a holiday—any holiday that you like. If you are working this exercise near the date of a holiday, you might want to use that holiday, but you can use one several months away if you like. Record in your Tarot journal the name of the Tarot deck that you'll be using, and the holiday.

What is the purpose of holidays, in your opinion? In your life, do holidays fulfill that purpose? What about this particular holiday? What is its purpose, in your opinion? Does it fulfill its purpose? In general? In your personal experience? Do you like this holiday? Dislike it? Have mixed feelings about it? Are you happy with your feelings about this holiday or would you prefer to have different feelings about it?

Go through your Tarot deck, faceup. Choose a card to represent how you feel about this particular holiday. Tell your journal how this card describes your feelings.

Go through your deck again, faceup. This time choose a card to represent how the general population seems to feel about this holiday. Explain how this card seems to describe the feelings of the general population.

Go through your deck yet a third time, faceup. This time choose a card that represents how you would like to feel about this holiday, how you would like to celebrate it. Explain why you have chosen this card.

You may use a card more than once if it fits more than one of these situations.

Are you happy with your choices, about what they say about personal and public holiday feelings? If so, you may stop the exercise now. If you would like to feel differently and/or would like the public to feel differently, then please continue.

Turn your deck over, facedown. Shuffle. Contemplate the question, "What do I need in my life to have a healthier, more enriching feeling or attitude about this holiday?" Choose a card facedown, in whatever manner is most comfortable to you. Turn the card over and look at it. What is the card? What does it seem to reveal to you as an answer to your question?

If you wish, you may also repeat this step with the following question, "What do we as a society need to have a healthier, more enriching feeling or attitude about this holiday?" Comment on this card choice as well.

What is a concrete step you can take to help you change your holiday experience, based on the cards that you have chosen? When will you take this step, and in what manner?

Goin' Home

I had this exercise in the back of my mind for several weeks before I wrote it. Many of these exercises were written quickly, in one sitting, but this is one that took some time, some research, and some input from my mother and from a good friend.

Once we've left home, we often have extremely mixed and conflicted feelings about going home again. Poet Robert Frost said that, "Home is the place where, when you have to go there, they have to take you in." Maybe. Maybe not. Some of us, no matter how desperate we are, would never go home again, at least not for anything other than a brief visit.

Novelist Thomas Wolfe expressed extremely different feelings when he said, "You can't go home again." And, you can't, not really. The home that you go back to is not the home that you left, and even if it was, you aren't the same person that left it.

Home is such an extremely complex and loaded concept that it is impossible to be objective. Even for those of us who have had difficult childhoods, the concept of home, if not the reality, still calls to us. Like Dorothy in Oz, we find that we just want to get home, even if home is dull and dreary. This yearning for home as concept (rather than reality) is poignantly portrayed in the classic movie *The Snake Pit*, starring Olivia de Havilland. Set in a women's mental hospital, it is a very disturbing movie. At one beautiful and heart-wrenching moment, the women in the hospital begin to sing the song "Goin' Home."

We know that the women in the mental hospital are not thinking of the reality of their home because a close reading of the lyrics shows that the song is really about going to heaven, not going to any physical home. Still, to the women in the movie, it was their idealized image of home that they wanted to go to. Most of us have an idealized image of home that we'd like to go home to as well, but life is not ideal, and home rarely lives up to our expectations.

This exercise is about dealing with our feelings and expectations about home. We come from a wide variety of homes. I hope that, no matter what kind of home you come from, you'll find this exercise helpful.

Choose a deck and go through your deck faceup. Set aside any cards that seem to depict your home in any form or fashion. Look at these cards carefully. Narrow your choices down to one to three cards. What are these cards and how do they picture your home?

Now, put the cards back in the deck and hold the deck in your hands. Think of the home you wish you'd had. Picture it in your mind. Make it concrete, with lots of details, whether you use a visual picture or detailed verbal description. (Not everyone can visualize pictures easily.)

Go through your deck faceup again, setting aside any cards that remind you of this ideal home. Narrow those choices down to one to three. What are they and how do they illustrate your concept of an ideal home, the home that you wish you'd had?

Interestingly, some of the cards may be the same.

Now, think of one really happy memory of home. Choose a card to match it. What is it? How does it fit your memory?

Think of one really painful memory of home. Choose a card to match it. What is it? How does it fit your memory?

Feel free to use new cards or cards that you've already used in this exercise.

Look carefully at the card that illustrates a painful memory of home. Go through your deck again, faceup, this time looking for a person or thing, idea, or action that would have helped in that painful time. What card did you choose? How would this have helped?

Look at the card that shows your happy memory of home. Does it have anything in common with the helpful card that you have just chosen? If so, what?

Do you ever go home in your current life? If so, what is going home like? Choose a card to illustrate what going home means to you today. If you don't go home physically, choose a card to illustrate what going home mentally means to you today—what does it mean to you to think about your home? Does it bother you? Make you anxious? Fill you with sorrow? With anger? Send you to the refrigerator to eat? Send you to the medicine cabinet to hunt for a sedative? Send you to a box of tissues because you start to cry? In other words, what card best shows how you feel about going home, either mentally or physically?

This is not the same as the card that represents your home. You could feel one way about the home of your past, but feel a different way about going home in your present life.

Going home may be good for you, or it may be difficult. It may be sorrowful, or it may be happy. No matter what going home means to you, no matter if you go home in memory or in action, think of one small concrete detail that you would like to change about going home. Choose a Tarot card to represent that detail. What is that detail? Resolve to take a deliberate concrete step toward changing that detail.

Maybe Later: An Exercise About Procrastination

I'm sure that no one reading this book has a problem with procrastination, but I do. Although I write very quickly and seldom do a great deal of editing or rewriting, I'll put off writing. I'll put off almost anything, and it's really strange when I find myself doing things that I normally put off in order to put off something else. For example, I normally procrastinate paying my bills. But I'll pay bills in order to procrastinate something else. I'll procrastinate doing laundry, but I'll do laundry in order to procrastinate doing something else. Procrastination is not logical. It defies logic, but it exists and sometimes it becomes a real problem, as I rediscovered while writing this book.

Think about a particular action or project that you are procrastinating about. This should be about a particular procrastination problem, not an overall problem with procrastination in general. What area of your life are you putting off until "maybe later"?

Choose your deck and go through your deck faceup, looking for a specific card to represent what you are procrastinating about. What is the card? How does it portray what you are procrastinating?

How do you feel about the card—in general, not when you are using it to describe what you are procrastinating about? How do you feel about the project that you are procrastinating about? How do you feel about this association between your task and the card?

Put the card back in the deck. Shuffle your deck. You will be choosing three cards, facedown. The first will represent your thoughts about the subject of your procrastination. The second will represent your emotions about your procrastination. The third will represent your actions (or inactions) about your procrastination. By whatever means is most comfortable for you, choose these three cards facedown: thoughts, emotions, actions.

What are the cards? Do they make sense to you? What do you discover about your procrastination by studying these three cards?

Finally, it is not enough to understand why we procrastinate. We must also act. Leave these three cards out of your deck. You are going to choose a final card to represent the best way to resolve your procrastination. Cut the deck. What card do you see in the cut? How can you use the energy of this card to devise an action to help you end the procrastination? Devise a concrete step, based on this card, which will be your first step in ending the procrastination. Do it as soon as possible. Now, if possible, rather than later.

Farewell

Often we have trouble letting go or saying goodbye. This tendency has many unhealthy results: staying overlong in negative relationships, holding on to a bad job, or being unable to let go of someone who has died, for instance. This is an exercise for saying farewell. Farewell is a bit different from goodbye. Goodbye has a note of finality to it: "This is the end." Farewell connotes that this is a departure, a time of leaving, but the option of getting back together in the future is still open, perhaps on another level, in another realm of existence.

Go through your deck faceup. Pull all of the cards that seem to say to you farewell or goodbye. Some of these cards will be rather extreme. Others will be mild. The cards that you choose will depend on the deck that you are using. In many decks, obvious choices will be Death, Judgement, 10 of Swords, the Wheel of Fortune, 8 of Cups, 6 of Swords, and the Moon. Choose these and any others that seem to say to you farewell.

Now, think of one particular area of your life where you are having trouble leaving or letting go. What is this area of your life? Choose a card face up to represent this area. What is it?

Now, look at your pile of farewell cards. In the best of all possible worlds, which farewell card would you choose to be the way for you to deal with this situation? In the worst of all possible worlds, which farewell card represents your worst nightmare about the situation?

You now have three cards. Put the others away. Put your best farewell card on the left, the card representing your current concern in the center, and the worst farewell card on the right.

Look carefully at all three cards. Study them closely. Take your time. Does anything jump out at you? If so, what is it?

Take a sheet of paper. Jot down your fears related to saying farewell to the situation. Taking markers or crayons or colored pencils, use colors or images from your worst farewell card to decorate the sheet of paper with your fears on it. Taking the necessary precautions, carefully burn this sheet of paper, saying, "I assign my fears over leaving this situation to the cleansing power of fire."

Take a second sheet of paper. Jot down all of the benefits to saying farewell to the situation. Use colors or images from your best farewell card to decorate this sheet of paper. Take a favorite incense, essential oil, or perfume. Anoint this sheet with a drop of aroma, saying, "I consecrate my intent to have a positive farewell for this situation with this aroma."

Based on the card of positive farewell, choose a concrete step that you can take toward saying farewell. What is that step? Put the card of positive farewell and your sheet of anointed paper together in a safe place until you have taken that step.

FIVE

SELF-DISCOVERY EXERCISE EXAMPLES

Sometimes it's helpful to see how others have worked the exercises. You can get an idea of the flexibility and power of the exercises and perhaps get inspiration to try some of the exercises that hadn't immediately appealed to you. In this chapter, we'll look at how a few people have worked the exercises. You'll see that they can be worked a variety of ways—powerfully, simply, seriously, or lightly. They can be worked by people with no experience with Tarot cards, and they can be worked by people with years of experience. They can be worked by the young and by the old. I'm constantly being surprised at how others use these exercises, and I'm sure that I'll continue to be surprised in the years to come.

All of the volunteers who worked the exercises were just given a copy of the exercise and then "turned loose." I didn't coach them, and, frequently, I wasn't even around when they worked the exercises. Most of the volunteers are friends and family members, but some are members of an e-mail list that I moderate. I'm even including three examples of exercises that I worked myself.

All of these exercises are described in full in the previous chapters in this book.

Who Am I? Example

Sometimes the exercises are very revealing about the person who works them, even when the exercise is short and the person has been brief in his or her answers. I asked a thirteen-year-old boy named Brad if he would work an exercise for me, more out of curiosity than anything else. Brad has seen Tarot cards and even had a reading or two from friends, but he had never studied or worked with the cards or even had a deck in his hands to play with before.

Brad didn't complete the exercise, but I was so bowled away by the parts of it that he did work that I want to share it with you. It reveals a lot about him and it surprised me.

I loaned Brad my *Robin Wood Tarot* for this exercise. To represent him at this moment, he chose the 3 of Swords. I was stunned! Brad is a bright, energetic, and outgoing person. His choice of cards completely surprised me. He says, "The card is a heart with three swords in it." The exercise asks, "What secrets about you does this card show?" Brad replied, "It shows that I'm upset, my pain at not seeing my girlfriend." To the question in the exercise, "What about you does the card omit?" Brad replied, "Nothing."

I've known Brad since he was seven. He's always had a string of girlfriends. Like most adults, I've sort of chuckled and then dismissed Brad's romances. After all, they were only kid's stuff, right? However, the 3 of Swords is a very powerful card. That Brad chose this card to represent himself tells me that, to him, his romances are very serious, very important. How well his romances are going impacts on his life in a bigger way than I would have dreamed.

Brad went on to say that he didn't want to be a different card, "because this card described me the best."

I was saddened to learn of Brad's pain, but, again, I was struck at the power of the Tarot cards to convey Brad's feelings and state of mind. From now on, I'll be more sensitive to Brad's romances and take him more seriously.

Tell Me a Story Example

Cindy, from my e-mail group, worked this sample exercise. It is one of the most amazing demonstrations of imagination that I've run across. In over two years of reading exercises written by others, this is one that is definitely unforgettable.

Method: shuffle and randomly, facedown, draw four cards. Use these cards to tell a story. Cindy used the *Spiral* deck and chose a character from the Temperance card to make a story about. This is her story:

> One late afternoon near the end of summer, Tammy Temperance was mixing up a batch of her favorite margarita recipe. While she was merrily blending (always shaking vigorously), she glanced out her kitchen window and noticed a man running down the beach. In his arms he was clutching a bundle of swords. He appeared to have an awful lot of them, and they kept threatening to slip out of his grasp. He seemed terribly nervous and distracted, and he kept looking behind himself—so much so that he didn't even notice the fox that was standing right in front of him.
>
> "A fox! What on earth? Where did that come from?" Tammy thought to herself. She gave her little cocktail a sip. "Hmm . . . more salt." Just then the nervous man with the swords sure enough ran right smack into that fox! Tripped, fell, swords went flying everywhere! The fox took off like a shot!
>
> "Oh good grief," mumbled Tammy. She hurried outside and down to the beach to offer her assistance. She was concerned the nervous fellow may have cut himself on the swords as he took a pretty nasty tumble.
>
> "Are you all right?" asked Tammy.
>
> "Oh yeah, sure, sure, I'm fine," said the nervous fella. "But my swords. . . ."
>
> Tammy was clueless but offered her assistance anyway. "Here let me help you up. My name is Tammy, Tammy

Temperance. I live in the house over behind the dunes.
Your swords are fine, just scattered a bit. Let me help you
get them up."

They walked about the dunes collecting the swords.

"My name is Nick," the nervous man finally said.

"Pleased to meet you, Nick," said Tammy, handing him
the last Sword.

Night was setting in, and Tammy offered to put Nick
up for the night, but he declined. Tammy got the feeling
Nick wasn't used to random acts of kindness. Feeling a
bit touched for him, she went up the house and returned
with some blankets, sandwiches, some sticks and matches,
and of course her jug of magical margarita heaven!

"Maybe this will help you to be more comfortable." She
started a little bonfire. Night had now engulfed the sky.
The Moon was out and in its full glory, its light dancing
atop the waters.

After a long silence, Nick got up and walked to the end
of the water. One by one he threw each and every sword
into the sea with all his might. Then he stood there just
looking up at the Moon in all its magical splendor. He
didn't say a word.

Tammy joined him at the water's edge. "She's quite
lovely tonight," she said. "What can you say about something so awesome?" now gazing upon the Moon herself.

"Yes, lovely," replied Nick, "and also very far away."
There was a sadness in his voice.

Together they walked back to the fire, After a few sips
of Tammy's famous margarita blend, Nick began to open
up to Tammy, telling her of his life—his dreams, his hopes,
but most of all his failures, and how he had gotten caught
up in a lifestyle he had never originally sought out. Times
were hard, and things just happen. Tammy listened intently
and with deep understanding.

When Nick had talked himself out, Tammy spoke up.
"I noticed you came running by earlier with all those

swords. Seemed to be all you could hold, and barely at that. But I also noticed that there were two left sticking in the sand, back in the direction you came from. Come, let's see if we can find them."

Nick declined. He did not want to go back. So Tammy went alone. She arrived back at their little camp a short while later, and, with her, two beautiful swords.

"Sharp and still very useful," she admired them. They nearly glowed in the light of the Moon. Tammy placed them between Nick and the fire.

"Nick, these belong to you," she said. "And you're not going to run with them, nor are you going to toss them in the sea. Sometimes, just sometimes Nick, we need to go back and claim what is ours. These are your swords, Nick, and tomorrow we are going to find a way to use them."

Nick just stared at Tammy. She was as soft and lovely and bright as the Moon above; within her she seemed to carry as much pull. How could he deny her? They drifted off to sleep.

Morning came, and as Nick opened his eyes, there stood Tammy holding his swords.

"Ready?" she asked.

What could he do? Nick got up and they began their journey down the beach until they arrived at the docks. Once there, Tammy scouted for, found, and introduced Nick to King Harold. King Harold was a merchant. He was specializing in the importing and exporting of exotic driftwood from around the world. It was becoming a very profitable business, not to mention increasingly demanding!

Tammy explained Nick's situation to King Harold.

"And since I've noticed that your workload has increased," Tammy went on, "I thought perhaps you could use a little help, and I believe that Nick here would make a fine apprentice."

Tammy was quite popular and influential in her water-front community, so King Harold listened to her. Still, he looked skeptical about the idea.

"He is very competent," continued Tammy, "and just look at his brilliant swords, and he did have more, once," Tammy shot a look at Nick.

King Harold was impressed with Nick's swords but still didn't see how they fit in with anything that Tammy was asking. Finally Tammy took King Harold to the side.

"Look Harry," she said, "what I'm saying here is give this guy a break, all right! Geez! Besides I've got a real good 'feeling' about him."

King Harold agreed, with the condition that this would be on an experimental basis, a project so to speak, and Tammy's project at that! But if it worked out well—well, King Harold could use a partner.

All three came then into agreement. They all came together and made a pact. Everyone got something: Nick, the opportunity he'd wanted for so long, the chance to show his real worth; King Harold, an assistant; and Tammy, the satisfaction of bringing the two together.

Nick became the most eager and determined worker King Harold had ever encountered. Harold grew to value him dearly. Nick went on to transform himself into a completely different person—organized, detailed, confident, and creative—why he even changed his name! He goes by Keith now, Keith Moon—the Moon part to always remind him of the night he shared with Tammy under that magical summer Moon.

Tammy visits Nick/Keith from time to time at the docks. She never really did check up on him like she promised Harold. But then again, she knew she'd never have to.

And Keith (now) often visits Tammy at her beachfront home, participating in what Tammy calls her "Magical Margarita Ritual."

The End

Featuring Temperance, 7 of Swords, Moon, 6 of Pentacles, and the Knight of Pentacles.

Eyes ready to fall out of your head yet? Less than a quarter of the way through, and I'd seen so much of my own life! I'd like to take the credit for being Tammy Temperance, but unfortunately, I'm Nick! I've learned so much about myself from this exercise that I couldn't even begin to list them all—the looking back and not seeing (fox) what's in front of you, the tossing of the swords, giving up the dreams you had hoped for, the reclaiming of the swords left—and that "someone," even if it is just that someone inside you that helps you move on, push forward, and not give up your dreams, not all together. I could pick this apart and go on and on . . . but I won't. I know what I got out of it, and I'm going to hold on to this for a long, long time. Whenever I feel like quitting. I'm going to pull this out and read it.

(*Note:* I heard from Cindy two years after she worked this exercise. She does still take it out from time to time and read it. All stories are true on some level. When we tell a story, if we look at it carefully, we always find truth, sometimes disturbing truth. Cindy's story is an excellent example of an entertaining story that holds great meaning for the storyteller.)

Life's Purpose Example

My daughter Katherine, seventeen years old at the time I'm writing this book, has provided the sample of the "Life's Purpose" exercise. Katherine has grown up surrounded by Tarot cards and various other metaphysical tools. She's familiar with a lot of them, but she's still a beginner with Tarot. For her exercise, she has chosen to use the *Voyager Tarot*.

> For the cards that reflect the desires and inspirations of her life, she chose the 10 of Wands, Fortune (Wheel of Fortune in other decks), the Sun, the 10 of Cups, Strength, and the Star.

The exercise says, "Look for common themes, symbols, and ideas in these cards." Katherine says, "Three of the cards have a hand in them. Four have flowers. Three have a type of flying bird. They all seem to have a sense of life's riches, worldly knowledge, and a more exterior sense than interior."

From these commonalities, Katherine says that a life purpose for her would be "perhaps something like my own creations will touch and enthrall people all around the world."

From a very early age, Katherine has been a very driven, focused, and ambitious person. She's a hard-working Capricorn with a Sagittarian Moon and Ascendant. It is entirely possible that she has accurately interpreted her life's purpose.

A Spirituality of My Own Example

This exercise was worked by my daughter Mary Frances, who was nineteen at the time that she worked it. I'm quite proud of both of my daughters, and as you read this example and the one worked by her sister, you can easily see why I'm so proud. Mary Frances used the *Robin Wood Tarot* deck for this exercise.

> At my spiritual void I was like the Fool because I was going on with my life fairly nonchalantly, believing that everything was all right. I had no idea just how empty I was inside and how much my spiritual void was affecting my life. The Fool is about to walk off a cliff, but she doesn't even realize it. This too is similar to me because when I headed down my current path, I could not predict me doing so beforehand, but I was like the Fool, walking along, only to be thrown into something that would shake up my life forever.
>
> For my spiritual past, I chose the Page of Wands and the 8 of Pentacles. When I was very little I attended a United Methodist Church, and as children tend to do, I

believed in everything I learned in Bible school with great awe and vigor. When I sang "Jesus Loves Me," let me tell you, Jesus *really* loved me. In the film *Dogma*, one character describes her faith as a small child, saying that maybe her spiritual cup as a youth was small, but it was brimming. That is an accurate description of me as well. I was truly touched in several ways, and this brought much passion into my early life.

When I was eight, however, my mother, my sister, and I began to attend a Unitarian Universalist church. It was a doctrine that I easily adopted, for my cup was beginning to empty as I was beginning to lose the blind acceptance of everything that my teachers and the little religious pamphlets told me. Growing up Unitarian Universalist, I worked hard, learning about multiple spiritual paths and ironing out a philosophy. I started to see spirituality as a craft, one that I studied with interest but did not apply to my own life. Like the 8 of Pentacles, I crafted many solid principles, but none of them affected me on a deeply spiritual level, leaving room for a spiritual void that began to creep into my life.

For my future spirituality I chose the 8 of Wands, the Queen of Wands, and the Star.

Automatic Response: I am hot fire shooting through the sky. I am hot and shining, moving quickly, a hot comet that will never burn out. My soul vacates my body and rises up, up into the sky where it belongs with all the other celestial bodies. I'm flying, I am one. My being curves around the air, letting Divinity run its hands over me and integrating me into it. I am one with them. It only makes me fly higher, going high, dipping low, but never stopping, always going, always growing. I'm bright, and I shine, and people down on earth below stop and stare as I illuminate the atmosphere and elevate even higher. I'm flying, and I know I'm never going to go down. I cannot

help but smile, a broad, true, smile, as I know my journey
has only begun and my path has no end. I look upon it
not with dread, but great anticipation of all the great
things that I can be.

Summary: I am something bright and moving through
the sky. I'm not stopping, but allowing my spirituality to
propel me higher. I'm a guide to others, but I am, most
importantly, an important, special being to myself.

I chose the Star as my one card for the future. To make
the Fool like the Star, I think she (or at least me) needs to
make working with her spirituality an everyday occur-
rence, so she can be as calm and majestic about it as the
Star. The Star handles her spirituality with great ease
because it is a basic part of her. That is the clear step I
want to take. I want my spirituality to be so integrated
into my life that it is a solid, outstanding part of me. As
for when? Why wait? I begin right now.

[*Note:* As awesome as this exercise is, Mary Frances neglected to
include a concrete step, which is a very important way to make her
intentions become reality.]

Lost in the Wasteland Example

I originally wrote this exercise for a special friend. I sent it to him in
e-mail, but he never worked it. When I began collecting sample exercises for this book, I asked him as a favor to me to work an exercise. I
gave him a list of the exercises that I was including, and he chose this
one. It is a rather grim and gloomy exercise, but I am glad that he
finally worked it. Here is what he reported:

I chose to work with the *Voyager Tarot* because I find it
very powerful in its imagery.

As for my current state of spirituality, I feel lost and
abandoned. I have tried so many beliefs and paths. All
paths seem to lead to the same dead end: disillusionment
and a loss of hope toward anything of a spiritual nature.
Yet I still harbor that grain of spiritual hope.

The main card that strikes me is the Hanged Man. To me it is a card of waiting and learning, suspended in space but not time, a card of reflection. The waiting stage is where I am again. This time it is harder because of the past. There are several things that strike me as a way to move forward in my spirituality.

First is the reflection shown on the card—I see the reflection as looking back over the past and learning from the mistakes and successes, a means to broaden the horizons using some of the valuable lessons I have learned. I see the hands holding the reflector as my hands, holding me up. I feel I must be capable of finding and maintaining my own spirituality.

Picking the reflection as my glimmer of hope, I chose the Sage of Crystals, 8 of Crystals, and the Man of Crystals as the cards to offer me guidance. [Note: In the *Voyager Tarot*, Crystals correspond, roughly, to the suit of Swords, Sages correspond roughly to Kings, and Men correspond roughly to Knights. The *Voyager Tarot* is a collage deck with many different images on each card.]

In the Sage of Crystals, I see Albert Einstein and a diamond which leads me to surmise that knowledge of the world and the self can lead me to know what I truly seek. It can help me build my foundation on the strongest rock in the world.

In the 8 of Crystals, I see the reflection in the clouds and a balancing act on a diamond, a balancing act of art and beauty and that of nature. I must learn to balance that which is my instinct with that which is society in order to be the foundation I desire to be.

In the Man of Crystals, I see the reflection of a man's face in a silicone chip, surrounded by scientific achievements of mankind. I see my next wave of spirituality as a combination of technology and spirituality, an inner and outer world of energy and learning experiences.

> I seem to find that to get out of my wasteland I need more education and need to experience the world of my inner thoughts and desires. To travel out, I need to travel inside. The reflection is me, but I am not the reflection.

My only note on this exercise is that the person failed to do a concrete step. I hope that he does find a concrete step and takes it soon.

Wedding Example

This is the first of three samples that I worked myself.

I'm using the *Robin Wood* 4 of Wands. I met my husband when he came to one of my Tarot workshops. He came to only one, and I didn't see him again for two months until he came to a psychic fair where I was doing readings. I was doing a free lecture on Tarot at the fair, and he attended it.

As a part of my presentation, I gave out cards from the Robin Wood deck. (I buy extra decks and give away cards during lectures or readings or whenever I feel like it.) In presentations such as this, I do an on-the-spot "snap" reading of the card that the person has chosen from my fanned out, facedown deck. Mike picked the 4 of Wands. Normally, in a situation like this, I would read the card as "public celebration," but for some reason on that day, I didn't. I said, "This card frequently represents marriage. Have you recently gotten married or are you thinking of getting married?" He shook his head "no," and I made some sort of comment like, "You may find yourself involved in a wedding or public celebration some time soon," and went on to the next person.

Soon after, Mike and I started to date, and this was "our" card. Just like some couples have a song, we had a Tarot card, the 4 of Wands.

> Have you ever attended a wedding that seemed to reflect this card? If so, tell us about it.
>
> My own wedding was not much like this card, but I have been to a wedding that was. In fact, I officiated at the wedding. Two friends of mine, Manderley and Michael (not to be confused with my husband Mike), got married

one summer in a brief, simple wedding. They had planned a big wedding a year in the future, but they decided not to wait and went ahead and had a legal wedding. They also went ahead with the big wedding on their original date, even though they were already legally married.

Their second wedding was the most amazing wedding that I have ever been to. Manderley, Michael, and I met several times to work out the ceremony, modifying the one that I usually use, adding to it, and rearranging it. I drove out to look at the site they had chosen (a state park), and we looked around to pick the best spot and decided where to hold the ceremony and where everyone would stand. Later, I went back for the actual rehearsal and the wedding itself.

The wedding was a masked wedding. We were encouraged to wear costumes and masks. I wore a dress that Manderley had made for my daughter when Katherine was in a school performance of *Ivanhoe*. It was a beautiful rose-colored brocade dress with a moss-green half cape. My friend Suzanne made me a mask out of leftover fabric from the dress. Manderley made her own dress as well as the bridesmaids' dresses (three), her mother-in-law's dress, and a dress for her cousin who sat at the guest book. Michael made his own kilt, peasant shirt, and leather belt.

Manderley also made all of the wedding favors herself, extra masks for guests who did not bring one, specially decorated paper tablecloths, corsages, signs showing the way to the wedding site, and about thirty decorative arrangements and centerpieces for the reception area and restrooms. In other words, her creative energies were everywhere. She is a professional artist, and everything was gorgeous and stunningly beautiful.

The bride and the groom were beautiful. Manderley looked like a fairy princess with her white dress, long red hair, dragonfly pins in her hair, and sparkle dust on her face and shoulders. Michael looked like a Scottish clan leader in his kilt and with his long hair. All of the grooms-men wore kilts. It was as close to a storybook wedding as I've ever seen.

In the wedding ceremony that you have described, who are you?

I am the minister. I was, in fact, the minister at this wedding, and this is how I see myself when I think of weddings these days.

Describe your wedding role as inspired by your Tarot card. How does this differ (or not differ) from how you normally see yourself?

In the weddings that I've done, I've always been the only minister. I would like to do a wedding with another minister. I would like to capture the essence of priest and priestess together in a marriage ceremony. As my concrete step, I have joined a local spiritual group and am involved in study and ritual. It is not quite what I want, but I hope that it will lead to what I truly want.

Bone Weary/Soul Weary Example

Tarot teacher and author Valerie Sim-Behi has used some of these exercises in her online Tarot class. She shared this example with me that was worked via e-mail by Harmony.

Harmony: I am using the *Rider* deck. The card that best fits how I feel when I am bone/soul weary is the 9 of Cups. When I feel so lost, so confused, so "why do I continue . . ." I find that I have sleepless nights, or worse yet nightmares. I can not find the solution and I can not let go of the problem. I am locked in a circle of grief, regret, anguish. This card with the person sitting up in their bed—no light about them, darkness only, hands holding the head, shoulders hunched—personifies the way I feel when I am bone/soul weary. This card fits my feelings so well, I can-not see a way in which it doesn't fit.

Valerie: I think perhaps you meant the 9 of Swords? If you did, this fits very well. This is beating oneself up repeatedly and carrying those thought processes into sleep, or lack of it. The important thing to understand is that your self-torture is magnifying the problem. Look at all those swords. How many are there? Nine? No! There is only one, it has merely been magnified repeatedly by the overwrought mind! When you look carefully at these swords you will realize that you have one saber that has mentally/emotionally been given greater power than it should have. Consciously dissipate the eight reflections and study the one real sword that is left. Is that easier to deal with now?

Harmony: The best card, as far as an aid goes for me, is the 2 of Cups. This card shows help in the form of someone you can trust. By sharing my concerns with another whose opinion I value, I can see the situation from another point of view. I can feel more sanguine that an answer can be found to the dilemma. or reassurance that I can make it through the hard times, even if an answer is not forthcoming. Sometimes just by having a listening ear, it is possible to see options I could otherwise close off from myself. If it falls short in any way, perhaps it is in the concern that by choosing the wrong confidante, I might not come up with my own answers, but rather follow theirs.

Valerie: Good! Now, sit quietly for a moment. How might you use the energy or skills or presence of this second Tarot card to avoid getting bone weary/soul weary in the future?

Harmony: Hmmm . . . the obvious answer to this is to make sure I seek out counsel before I get too far into a situation. Or maybe the answer is as simple as listening when someone tells me I seem too preoccupied and/or don't look well. It is too easy to keep moving forward and not realize that without occasional breaks, we run the risk of "burning the candle at both ends."

Valerie: Yes, and keep in mind that we actually create our own horrors by dwelling on them. Don't put energy into manifesting your nightmares, but rather seek counsel and that listening ear to guide you in investing energy into creating a positive reality.

Think of a concrete step you could take the next time you start to get tired that would help you avoid the overwhelming bone weary/soul weary tiredness. What is that step? Choose a Tarot card to represent that step.

Harmony: The Hanged Man is probably the best step to take. It seems to me that there are times when I need to just step back, take a breather and look at things from a different point of view. By using the Hanged Man aspects, I can choose to pull back before I am overwhelmed by circumstances beyond my control. Taking that pause, and seeing things from a new perspective may keep me from arriving at that 9 of Swords spot.

Prosperity and Abundance Example

I not only write Tarot for Self-Discovery exercises, I also sometimes work them as well. This is the first exercise that I wrote, and it is the first one of my own that I worked. I pulled it out from my notes as I was in the finishing stages of my book and was bowled over by it. You see, I worked this exercise more than two years before I worked the "Maybe Later" exercise. I've provided my working of that exercise as well, later in this chapter. When I noticed the similarities between the two exercises, I became more convinced than ever of the power of the Tarot to transmit powerful messages to us. The only trouble that I have is in sometimes listening to those messages and making the appropriate changes in my life.

I have my *Robin Wood Tarot* before me, going through it, faceup, trying to pick a card that represents to me "prosperity, wealth, abundance, and plenty." I had to set aside my mental knowledge of the deck and use just my reactions to the pictures on the cards. I know, for instance, which cards mean abundance and plenty and prosperity and wealth. However, for this exercise, I need to use a card that at this moment visually speaks to me of those qualities.

I am amazed at my choices. When I do exercises like this, I normally choose several cards and then narrow things down to one card. In this case, my first choices are quite interesting: Judgement, Ace of Pentacles, 6 of Wands, the Sun, 3 of Wands, Knight of Pentacles, Page of Pentacles, the Star, Queen of Pentacles, the World, Queen of Cups, 2 of Cups, the Magician, Ace of Cups, and King of Cups. I am surprised at the number of cups cards. How interesting.

This says to me that perhaps emotional abundance is more important to me than material abundance. After some thought, I narrow my choices down to the 6 of Wands and the Queen of Cups. It is a difficult decision, but I finally go with the Queen of Cups. My choices would be different with a different deck, but in this deck at this moment, this is the card that speaks to me most of prosperity and abundance.

I see on this card a regal woman sitting in a beautiful shell chair, with the sunrise at her shoulder, looking at a goblet that she holds before her.

The parts of the card that make me think specifically of abundance, plenty, prosperity, and wealth are the woman's robes, her chair, being able to afford a private ocean view, her ornately decorated hair, her serenity. Her robe is getting wet in the ocean—and she's not worried about ruining it.

The colors are rich and lush. There is a lot of purple, and purple makes me think of riches because early purple dye was very rare and restricted to royalty. Therefore purple is a rare and costly color to wear.

> *My story:* "Wealthy recluse spotted at her island retreat."
> The Queen of Cups, wealthiest woman in the world, has
> been spotted on the beach of her island retreat. Normally
> extremely private, the Queen is elusive and hard to see.

She was spotted on the beach, taking a morning cup of her favorite beverage by the sea. Although she noticed the photographers and reporters, she remained serene and confident. She appeared to be enjoying the company of sea lions and sea gulls as she watched the sunrise. When she had finished her morning beverage, she turned, stretched, smiled, and walked back to her home.

Retell the story with me as the main character: I was spotted at my island retreat. I, the wealthiest woman in the world, was seen on the beach of my island retreat. Normally extremely private, I am elusive and hard to see. I was spotted on the beach, taking a morning cup of my favorite beverage (Diet Dr. Pepper) by the sea. Although I saw the photographers and reporters, I remained serene and confident. I was enjoying the company of sea lions and sea gulls as I watched the sunrise. When I finished my morning beverage, I turned, stretched, smiled, and walked back to my home.

What message does this give to me about my attitudes toward prosperity? Well, to me, prosperity involves being able to have privacy, to be able to be alone, to be able to live in a quiet and secluded area. It also includes having people want to see me, so there is a strong polarity of privacy versus being in the public eye for me in wealth and prosperity issues.

Also, in the story, the Queen and I are the ones in control of the situation, so I think that prosperity, to me, is associated with having some control over one's surroundings.

What ideas does this give me about improving my prosperity? I'm not sure. Getting seen more, possibly, but without giving up my privacy, which I obviously cherish highly.

Maybe Later Example

I worked this exercise as I was dealing with finishing this book. I was past my deadline at the time of the working.

Think about a particular action or project that you are procrastinating about.

Writing my book. I should have finished it a couple of weeks ago. I've had problems—unexpected house guests, computer woes, a sinus infection, but, honestly, I could have finished it. There is really only a little bit left, a very little bit. It's not that it's taking longer than I thought it would (although there is a bit of that involved), but that I am just avoiding working on the book. If I would just do the work, I could finish very quickly.

Choose your deck. Tell us the name of your deck.
Universal Waite.

Go through your deck faceup, looking for a specific card to represent what you are procrastinating about. What is the card?

The Ace of Swords. To me, Swords are writing and communications. Aces are beginnings and firsts. A first book (which this is, for me) was a clear Ace of Swords at the time that I worked this exercise. [Note: Upon reflection, it seems that a different choice might have been better, something to indicate finishing, not beginning. In the *Universal Waite* deck, I would choose the Hermit to indicate finishing the book.]

How do you feel about the card—in general, not when you are using it to describe what you are procrastinating about?

I like this card. It is nothing terribly exciting in the *Universal Waite* deck, but overall I like the meaning a great deal and find it a positive and affirming card. The concept of the card is exciting because I am thrilled by communicating and knowledge.

How do you feel about the project that you are procrastinating about?

Well, this is interesting. I am very ambivalent about the book. I write quickly and fairly well. However, I don't enjoy writing in a vacuum. Writing e-mail is fun because of the quick feedback, but writing a book is delayed gratification, which is rougher. I never really wanted to be a writer, never really wanted to write a book. However, I do want to teach and travel and speak, and, to me, writing books is an important part of that overall desire/plan. People are much more likely to invite you to travel, to come to a conference and give a talk, if you have a few books out there. So, I am writing a book as a means to an end not necessarily a desired end in itself.

Also, many, many people have asked me to write a book. When I told some of them that I was working on this book, they were very excited, much more so than I was. So, in part, I am writing this book for others.

Thirdly, I have learned the hard way that I do not do well working in a typical office setting. I need a great deal of privacy in order to maintain my personal sanity. If I don't get enough private time, I begin to shut down— mentally, emotionally, and spiritually. Writing is an occupation that provides a great deal of privacy, so although writing itself is not a joy, I don't dislike it, and it has many positive qualities for me—a means to a desired end, a way to gratify others, and a job that provides necessary privacy.

Finally, I did sign a contract. I am already overdue. I do try to meet my obligations, and since I have signed a contract, I need to get this book finished in order not to feel guilty for the rest of my life.

How do you feel about this association between your task and the card?

Good.

By whatever means is most comfortable for you, choose these three cards face down—thoughts, emotions, actions.

Thoughts: 9 of Cups; Emotions: 9 of Pentacles; Actions: Page of Pentacles.

The 9 of Cups indicates that it is indeed my wish to finish the book. I do want to get it done. However, I am also feeling a bit overwhelmed at the prospect. In part, I do not feel worthy of being an author. The 9 of Pentacles, to me, really really emphasizes my recent privacy deprivation. The woman in the 9 of Pentacles is alone in her garden, and she really loves it there. I really love being alone as well. As someone who lives with a family, however, my privacy is rare and cherished. If I am at home during the day when the others are at work and school, I can achieve privacy. This is the main reason that I quit my day job. However, unfortunately, I did it during the summer, so my children are still at home a lot (although they are teenagers with part-time jobs). Still, my lack of privacy and my almost total shutdown, to me, are a real and even legitimate reason for procrastination. My procrastination went beyond this, though.

The Page of Pentacles was the hardest card for me to interpret. The Page of Pentacles is the student of the deck and may be a bit insecure because he is doing something new. A part of me is fearful and insecure about writing a book. I've written thousands and thousands of words on the internet and in email for years on the subject of Tarot. Still, I've never written a book. I am even a dropout as an author. I was working on a Ph.D. in English, and I got all of the way done except for the dissertation. I was unable to finish the dissertation. Part of me wonders, "Can I finish a book at all?" However, I know that I can finish this one. I only got about half done with the first draft of the dissertation. I am about 90 percent or more finished with this book. I do think that my past failure at writing a book is part of the problem, especially since I was writing the book as a student and this is a student card.

Finally, it is not enough to understand why we procrastinate. We must also act. Leave these three cards out of your deck. You are going to choose a final card to represent the best way to resolve your procrastination. Cut the deck. What card do you see in the cut?

I had to laugh when I saw this card—the 8 of Pentacles. This is the person working at his craft. The message to me was clear: Just do it.

My concrete step was to begin writing the next day at 10 A.M. and to write for two to four hours that day on the book. I got up. I worked on the book at 10 A.M. for about an hour and took a break, and I didn't go back to the book for over a week. As I learned all too well, devising the concrete step is not enough. Starting the concrete step is not enough. Making sure that you do the concrete step or revise it so that it can be done is what counts.

What I found, and I am getting extremely personal here, is that I was addicted to a computer game. I had started playing it during my shutdown time. I would come home from work and play my game for hours. It was my coping mechanism, my crutch. It got me through the hard times. When I quit my job, I played my game for about five days, nonstop, and then I put it away and began work on my talk for an American Tarot Association conference and began working on the book.

When I had my first set of unexpected house guests, I found that I was unable to get quiet time to work on my book. So, I pulled out my computer game and started playing it. I became hooked again. No matter that I had resolved in my concrete step to work at 10 A.M. every day for two to four hours, I was unable to follow through. So, I had to think again. How can I carry through my concrete step?

My answer was to find some way that I would be unable to play my computer game during part of the day.

I write at the computer, so I would need access to my computer, but my game requires that a CD/ROM be in the CD drive while I play. I decided to ask my husband if he would take my game CD to work with him each day so that I would be unable to play my game. This worked. I got jumpy and edgy at not having my game, but I still managed to finish the book. When my husband came home at night, he brought my CD, and I played for a while before I went to bed. I had thought about asking him to keep the CD until I finished the book, but this seemed extreme. I feared that I would come to resent the book for coming between me and my game. By only playing the game in the evenings and weekends, I still had my pleasure, but I was also able to focus during the workday on writing.

SIX

WRITING YOUR OWN SELF-DISCOVERY EXERCISES

hat happens if you've looked over all of the exercises in *Tarot for Self Discovery*, and you can't find one that meets your needs or wants? You could try writing an exercise yourself.

Here are some suggestions for writing self-discovery exercises using the Tarot.

Have a need that you are trying to meet. Want to try and figure out how to get out of an emotional rut? Want some help dealing with a difficult relationship? Want to increase your job satisfaction? Any and all of these problems can be addressed through a self-discovery exercise. However, one exercise cannot solve all of your problems. Take a need, a problem, an issue, and focus on it.

Remember that you are trying to learn something about yourself and possibly also about others. What is the best way to discover these insights?

Break down your ideas into small, easy-to-understand steps. Take each step in order. Don't get too complex. If you must get complex (and sometimes you do), make sure that each step is simple and clear. A complex exercise can be clear if all of the steps are clear.

1 Limit the number of cards with which you work

2 Decide if you want to choose cards faceup or facedown
   during the exercise—this can be important; choosing faceup
   has one set of subtle reactions and choosing facedown has
   another set of subtle reactions; faceup works more with
   your subconscious, with getting at what's hidden in your
   own psyche; facedown deals more with chance and fate,
   and getting direction from outside of yourself

3 Think about how long it will take to work the exercise. An
   exercise can be long or short, but even a long exercise should
   be do-able in one afternoon; if your exercise seems to be
   achieving a life of its own, seems to becoming a life's work
   and not an afternoon's work, then revise it

4 Include a part about really looking at a card and/or really
   thinking about a card

5 Connect the card in some way to your life in one or more of
   the steps

Here are some suggestions for exercises for others to work, not just
yourself.

How will you introduce the exercise to us? Sometimes I start an
exercise off with a little anecdote, telling how I got the idea for the
exercise or targeting the kinds of life issues that can most benefit from
this particular exercise.

Close with a concrete step, if appropriate.

In addition, I look to life and music for inspiration. What areas of
my life am I having trouble with? What areas of life are my friends and
family having trouble with? What songs are on my mind? What new
concepts and ideas am I trying to explore? I used all of these and more
as inspiration for writing the *Tarot for Self Discovery* exercises and perhaps they will be inspiration for you as well.

INTRODUCTION TO CHAKRAS

Briefly, we have energy centers in our bodies which some people call chakras. There are over two hundred of these energy centers, but most students of chakras agree that there are seven major ones aligned along the center of the body. A basic working knowledge of the seven major chakras comes in handy in all sorts of metaphysical work. There are chakra spreads to use in Tarot. There are correspondences between the seven major chakras and the seven ancient planets in astrology. Reiki and Tai Chi and aura work all benefit from knowledge of the chakras. Chakras are often pictured as glowing colored lotus petals, and, indeed, each chakra has been assigned a distinctive petal pattern and color and additional shapes.

You can view the chakras as symbolic or physical, or a combination of both. When I first started running into the concept of chakras, I was extremely skeptical. However, a little bit of work with chakras was all that it took for me to overcome much of my skepticism. If you want to know more about the esoteric meanings and uses of the chakras, I recommend *Wheels of Life* by Anodea Judith and *Anatomy of the Spirit* by Caroline Myss.

The first chakra, or root chakra, is located at the base of the spine. It is the chakra of survival and grounding, and is called *Muladhara* in Sanskrit. It is associated with the color red. When this chakra is malfunctioning, there may be symptoms of obesity, hemorrhoids, constipation, sciatica, degenerative arthritis, anorexia nervosa, and knee troubles.

The second chakra, or sacral chakra, is located in the lower abdomen, about two inches below the naval. It is the chakra of desire, pleasure, and sexuality and is called *Svadhisthana* in Sanskrit. It is associated with the color orange. When this chakra is malfunctioning, there may be symptoms of impotence, frigidity, stiff lower back, or uterine, bladder, or kidney trouble. This chakra is also connected to money.

The third chakra, or solar plexus, is located at the diaphragm. This is our power center, and it is the chakra of the will. It is also known as *Manipura*. Most people are extremely aware of their solar plexus. When you feel strong, this is where you will feel your strength radiating from. When you feel weak, you'll often feel nausea radiating from the solar plexus. The solar plexus is associated with the color yellow. When this chakra is malfunctioning, there may be symptoms of ulcers, diabetes, hypoglycemia, indigestion, hepatitis, and liver problems.

The fourth chakra is the heart chakra, located in the center of the chest. The heart chakra is the chakra of love and healing, called *Anahata* in Sanskrit. The color for the heart chakra is green. When this chakra is malfunctioning, there may be problems of asthma, high blood pressure, heart disease, and lung disease.

The fifth chakra is the throat chakra, located in the center of the throat. It is the chakra of communication and creativity, *Visuddha* in Sanskrit. The color for the throat chakra is blue. When this chakra is malfunctioning, there may be problems with a sore throat, stiff neck, colds, thyroid problems, hearing problems.

The sixth chakra is often called the psychic eye. It is located between the eyebrows in the center of the lower forehead. It is the chakra of seeing and intuition, called *Ajna* in Sanskrit. The color for the psychic eye is indigo in many systems, but some systems use violet. When this chakra is malfunctioning, there may be problems with eyesight, headaches, and nightmares.

The seventh chakra is the crown chakra. Depending on the source that you use, it is either at the top of the head or about two inches above the top of the head. It is the chakra of understanding and is called *Sahasrara* in Sanskrit. The color for the crown chakra is violet in many systems, but some systems use white. When this chakra is malfunctioning, there may be problems with depression, alienation, confusion, boredom, apathy, an inability to learn or comprehend.

With this short introduction, you should have enough information about chakras to be able to do the "Chakra Dance" exercise on page 45.

CRASH COURSE IN ASTROLOGY

A natal chart is comprised of four main components: planets, signs, houses, and aspects. Most people who are astrological novices know only of the twelve signs. They may or may not know the basic characteristics of each sign. In astrology, we also use ten planets (the Sun, Moon and the planets except for Earth) and twelve houses. There are resonances or correlations between these three: signs, planets, and houses. As a gross oversimplification, I could say that there are twelve basic flavors in astrology and three main expressions of each flavor. Just as there are many different ways to experience chocolate, there are several different ways to experience Scorpio in a chart. You don't have to be a Scorpio for Scorpio energy to be prominent in your chart. If you feel like a Leo but aren't a Leo, it's probably because some other part of your chart has strong Leo resonances. Let's look at the different flavors or resonances of simplified astrology.

- Aries resonates with Mars and the first house

- Taurus resonates with Venus and the second house

- Gemini resonates with Mercury and the third house

- Cancer resonates with the Moon and the fourth house
- Leo resonates with the Sun and the fifth house
- Virgo resonates with Mercury and the sixth house
- Libra resonates with Venus and the seventh house
- Scorpio resonates with Pluto and the eighth house
- Sagittarius resonates with Jupiter and the ninth house
- Capricorn resonates with Saturn and the tenth house
- Aquarius resonates with Uranus and the eleventh house
- Pisces resonates with Neptune and the twelfth house

To get the Aries flavor in a chart, you can have one or more planets in Aries, Aries on one of the four angles (Ascendant—especially the Ascendant, Descendant, Midheaven, and IC), planets in the first house, or a strongly placed Mars.

To get the Taurus flavor in a chart, you can have one or more planets in Taurus, Taurus on one of the four angles (Ascendant—especially the Ascendant, Descendant, Midheaven, and IC), planets in the second house, or a strongly placed Venus.

To get the Gemini flavor in a chart, you can have one or more planets in Gemini, Gemini on one of the four angles (Ascendant—especially the Ascendant, Descendant, Midheaven, and IC), planets in the third house, or a strongly placed Mercury.

To get the Cancer flavor in a chart, you can have one or more planets in Cancer, Cancer on one of the four angles (Ascendant—especially the Ascendant, Descendant, Midheaven, and IC), planets in the fourth house, or a strongly placed Moon.

To get the Leo flavor in a chart, you can have one or more planets in Leo, Leo on one of the four angles (Ascendant—especially the Ascendant, Descendant, Midheaven, and IC), planets in the fifth house, or a strongly placed Sun.

To get the Virgo flavor in a chart, you can have one or more planets in Virgo, Virgo on one of the four angles (Ascendant—especially the

Ascendant, Descendant, Midheaven, and IC), planets in the sixth house, or a strongly placed Mercury.

To get the Libra flavor in a chart, you can have one or more planets in Libra, Libra on one of the four angles (Ascendant—especially the Ascendant, Descendant, Midheaven, and IC), planets in the seventh house, or a strongly placed Venus.

To get the Scorpio flavor in a chart, you can have one or more planets in Scorpio, Scorpio on one of the four angles (Ascendant—especially the Ascendant, Descendant, Midheaven, and IC), planets in the eighth house, or a strongly placed Pluto.

To get the Sagittarius flavor in a chart, you can have one or more planets in Sagittarius, Sagittarius on one of the four angles (Ascendant—especially the Ascendant, Descendant, Midheaven, and IC), planets in the ninth house, or a strongly placed Jupiter.

To get the Capricorn flavor in a chart, you can have one or more planets in Capricorn, Capricorn on one of the four angles (Ascendant—especially the Ascendant, Descendant, Midheaven, and IC), planets in the tenth house, or a strongly placed Saturn.

To get the Aquarius flavor in a chart, you can have one or more planets in Aquarius, Aquarius on one of the four angles (Ascendant—especially the Ascendant, Descendant, Midheaven, and IC), planets in the eleventh house, or a strongly placed Uranus.

To get the Pisces flavor in a chart, you can have one or more planets in Pisces, Pisces on one of the four angles (Ascendant—especially the Ascendant, Descendant, Midheaven, and IC), planets in the twelfth house, or a strongly placed Neptune.

Remember, this is a gross simplification of astrology, but it should suffice to help you understand enough astrology to understand the exercises in this book. Signs and houses and planets are not equal, are not equivalent, but they do share a lot of the same qualities. Therefore, the house and planet associated with a sign will have common features. For example, Libra is ruled by Venus, the planet of love and art, and has its native house as the seventh house. Libras are notorious romantics, and the seventh house is the house of marriage and partnerships. Venus is not Libra is not the seventh house, but there is a commonality to them all.

It is helpful to think of your natal chart as a road map for your life. It is the road map for the "Best Possible You." It is also the roadmap for "Everything That Can Possibly Go Wrong." By working with the information in our charts about ourselves, we can live our lives in a much more healthy and happy way.

There needs to be a balance of the various parts of your chart. Suppose that one part of your chart screams "mothering, nurturing, homebody" (as mine does) and another part of your chart screams "get on stage, show off, get attention" (as mine does). If you ignore either voice, you are asking for trouble. You have to learn how to do both—how to feed the energies of both parts of yourself.

In a way, your natal chart is a description of your weaknesses and a description of your strengths. When the different parts of a chart fight with each other, their weaknesses are emphasized. When they work together in respect and harmony, their strengths are emphasized. No one component should be sacrificed. All are important. All are essential.

Should you ignore your Sun, your essence, and live only for your Ascendant and Moon, then you would be prey to depression or despair or being only partly alive. Should you try to ignore the Moon, you would be insecure and unstable. You need that part of your personality. All are necessary, even when they don't seem to work together easily. You *can* decorate a room in green, red, and violet, but it takes great skill and a willingness to take chances.

Except for the Moon, most, if not all of the planets will not change time during the course of a single day, so, for most people, the time of day and location of birth is not important just to know the sign that each particular planet is in except for the Moon, which is a very big exception since it is a major force in our lives and in astrological study.

The houses are the part of the chart that is totally dependent on the birth time and place, and, with the houses, the various angles of the chart—the Ascendant, Descendant, Midheaven, and IC. The signs and planets on or near your angles play an important part in the total interpretation of your chart. If your birth time is estimated and is off only five minutes or so from the actual time, there is likely to be very little significance, but if you are off by an hour or so, the difference can be substantial. It is normally best to go by official records whenever possible rather than by family memories which can be vague or inaccurate. For instance, my own mother remembers my birth time as "about 8:30" P.M. According to official records, I was born at 7:48 P.M. This is only forty-two minutes, but it made a difference of nine degrees on my Ascendant and would have indicated a Gemini Ascendant rather than the Cancer Ascendant which I really have.

These small differences of degree can be significant, so before you go any further, please try and find an accurate time of birth. Do not give up on astrology if you cannot find out your birth time, but you should make a strong effort to find your correct time. The uses that we have for astrology in this book do rely on accurate birth information.

How does a chart work? Why are houses important? A chart with five planets in the fifth house (House of Creativity, Romance, and Children) will be quite different from a chart with five planets in the twelfth house (House of Sorrow and Suffering). A person with an active fifth house can expect to have the issues of children, creativity, and romance prominent in his or her life. The twelfth house is the house of limitations, the subconscious, hidden strengths, endings, and sorrows or frustrations. Five planets in the twelfth house would indicate a very different kind of life from five planets in the fifth.

You begin reading an astrological chart at the nine o'clock position. This an angle called the Ascendant. It is also the cusp of the first house. The sign on the cusp of the first house is often called the Rising Sign. Therefore, the sign that you have beginning the first house, at the nine o'clock position, is your rising sign, the sign on your Ascendant.

By carefully looking at a chart you can decipher all of those strange glyphs with very little help.

There are many correspondences between Tarot and astrology. In fact, there are several different systems that formalize the various correspondences between the two disciplines. One of the more popular and widely known of these systems is the one used by the Golden Dawn, a mystery school that flourished during the late nineteenth century and early twentieth century.

According to astrology, each sign has a planetary ruler. According to the Golden Dawn system, each sign and each planet have a corresponding Tarot card.

In an individual's personal chart, any sign might be in any house. Aries might be in the first house or the fifth house, the eighth or the eleventh. Putting aside for a moment the concept of individual charts, each of the twelve houses in astrology has a "native" or "home base" or favored sign associated with it, so that no matter what sign is in that house in a person's chart, the house also carries with it the influences or characteristics of that sign. Aries always flavors the first house in some way. Taurus always flavors the second house, and so forth. It is this association that you sometimes see pictured on a blank chart or a study chart.

In order to work some of the exercises in this book, you will need to consult the table below to find the Tarot card that corresponds to a planet or sign. Here is a list of the houses, colors, signs, planets, and their corresponding Tarot cards according to the Golden Dawn system, which is the one that I prefer.

House	Area	Color	Sign, Card	Ruling Planet, Card
First	Personality	Red	Aries, Emperor	Mars, Tower
Second	Money	Red-orange	Taurus, Hierophant	Venus, Empress
Third	Communication	Orange	Gemini, Lovers	Mercury, Magician
Fourth	Home	Yellow-orange	Cancer, Chariot	Moon, High Priestess
Fifth	Pleasure	Yellow	Leo, Strength	Sun, Sun
Sixth	Servants	Yellow-green	Virgo, Hermit	Mercury, Magician
Seventh	Marriage	Green	Libra, Justice	Venus, Empress
Eighth	Death	Green-blue	Scorpio, Death	Pluto, Judgement
Ninth	Philosophy	Blue	Sagittarius, Temperance	Jupiter, Wheel of Fortune
Tenth	Career	Blue-violet	Capricorn, Devil	Saturn, World
Eleventh	Goals	Violet	Aquarius, Star	Uranus, Fool
Twelfth	Sorrows	Red-violet	Pisces, Moon	Neptune, Hanged Man

APPENDIX C

THE GOLDEN DAWN

The Hermetic Order of the Golden Dawn flourished in England from 1888 until 1903. After that time, its influence continued to grow through various offshoots. Some prominent groups that have connections to the Hermetic Order of the Golden Dawn include Builders of the Adytum (B.O.T.A.), Servants of Light, Fraternity of Hidden Light, Society of Inner Light, Holy Order of the Golden Dawn, and Ordo Templi Orientis (O.T.O.). The Golden Dawn was an esoteric group that combined various occult sciences into one system of study. Its members were intelligent, imaginative, and dedicated people who worked and studied hard to use esoteric tools as an aid to spiritual growth.

I refer to the Golden Dawn in this book because their system of correspondences is the best-known system, and I have found its system of correspondences to be very workable. I actually use (and include in this book) a variation on their system of correspondences that is taught by B.O.T.A. Many Tarot decks are designed around this system of correspondences, and if you become familiar with this system, it can aid in your understanding of these decks. There are other systems of correspondences that work well, and you are free to use whatever system you prefer when you are working these exercises. It is important to find (or devise) a system that you like and to be consistent in its use.

If you wish to know more about the Golden Dawn, I refer you to the many fine books on the Golden Dawn written by Chic and Sandra Tabatha Cicero and published by Llewellyn Worldwide.

BIBLIOGRAPHY

Almond, Jocelyn, and Keith Seddon. *Understanding Tarot: A Practical Guide to Tarot Card Reading.* London: Aquarian-HarperCollins, 1991.

Arrien, Angeles. *The Tarot Workbook.* Sonoma, California: Arcus Publishing, 1984.

Bartlett, John. *Bartlett's Familiar Quotations,* 5th ed. Boston: Little Brown, 1980.

Budapest, Zsuzsanna. *The Holy Book of Women's Mysteries* (Complete in One Volume). 1980, 1986. Oakland, California: Wingbow, 1989.

Butler, Bill. *The Definitive Tarot.* London: Century Hutchinson, 1975. Rpt. as *Dictionary of the Tarot.* New York: Pantheon-Random House, 1975.

Campbell, Joseph, and Richard Roberts. *Tarot Revelations.* 1982. San Anselmo, California: Vernal Equinox Press, 1987.

Douglas, Alfred. *The Tarot: The Origins, Meaning and Uses of the Cards.* 1972. Harmondsworth, England: Penguin, 1973.

Emerson, Ralph Waldo. "Self Reliance." *Selections from Ralph Waldo Emerson.* Ed. Stephen E. Whicher. Boston: Houghton Mifflin, 1960.

Forrest, Steven. *The Inner Sky.* San Diego, California: ACS Publications, 1989.

Gearhart, Sally, and Susan Rennie. *A Feminist Tarot.* Rev. ed. Boston: Alyson, 1981.

Giles, Cynthia. *The Tarot: History, Mystery and Lore.* New York: Paragon House, 1992.

Gray, Eden. *A Complete Guide to the Tarot.* Toronto: Bantam-Crown, 1970.

———. *Mastering the Tarot.* New York: Signet-Crown, 1971.

Greer, Mary K. *Tarot Constellations: Patterns of Personal Destiny.* North Hollywood, California: Newcastle Publishing, 1987.

———. *Tarot for Your Self: A Workbook for Personal Transformation.* North Hollywood, California: Newcastle Publishing, 1984.

Jayanti, Amber. *Living the Tarot.* St. Paul, Minnesota: Llewellyn, 1993.

Judith, Anodea. *Wheels of Life: A User's Guide to the Chakra System.* St. Paul, Minnesota: Llewellyn, 1993.

Kaplan, Stuart R. *The Encyclopedia of Tarot.* 3 vols. Stamford, Connecticut: U.S. Games Systems, 1978-1990.

Knight, Gareth. *The Treasure House of Images: An Introduction to the Magical Dynamics of the Tarot.* Rochester, Vermont: Destiny Books, 1986.

Lauter, Estella. *Women as Mythmakers: Poetry and Visual Art by Twentieth-Century Women.* Bloomington, Indiana: UP, 1984.

Lotterhand, Jason. *The Thursday Night Tarot.* North Hollywood, California: Newcastle Publishing, 1989.

March, Marion D., and Joan McEvers. *The Only Way to Learn Astrology,* Vol. 1: Basic Principles. San Diego, California: ACS Publications, 1980.

Merriam-Webster's Collegiate Dictionary, 10th ed. Springfield, Massachusetts: Merriam-Webster, 1995.

Myss, Caroline. *Anatomy of the Spirit: The Seven Stages of Power and Healing.* New York: Three Rivers Press, 1996.

O'Neill, Robert V. *Tarot Symbolism.* Lima, Ohio: Fairway Press, 1986.

Pollack, Rachel. *Seventy-eight Degrees of Wisdom: A Book of Tarot Part I: The Major Arcana.* Wellingborough, England: Aquarian, 1980.

Porter, Cole. "You're the Top." Harms, Inc., 1934.

Rogers-Gallagher, Kim. *Astrology for the Light Side of the Brain.* San Diego, California: ACS Publications, 1995.

Waite, Arthur Edward. *The Pictorial Key to the Tarot.* 1910. York Beach, Maine: Samuel Weiser, 1989.

Waite, Arthur Edward, and Pamela Colman Smith. *The Rider Tarot Deck.* 1910. Stamford, Connecticut: U.S. Games Systems, 1971.

Wang, Robert. *Qabalistic Tarot: A Textbook of Mystical Philosophy.* York Beach, Maine: Samuel Weiser, 1983.

Wood, Robin. *The Robin Wood Tarot.* St. Paul, Minnesota: Llewellyn, 1995.

The Complete Book of Tarot Reversals

Mary K. Greer

The topsy-turvy world of upside-down cards

What do you do with the "other half" of a Tarot reading: the reversed cards? Just ignore them as many people do? *Tarot Reversals* reveals everything you need to know for reading the most maligned and misunderstood part of a spread. These interpretations offer inner support, positive advice, and descriptions of the learning opportunities available, yet with a twist that is uniquely their own.

Enhance and deepen the quality of your consultations as you experiment with the eleven different methods of reading reversed cards. Use the author's interpretations to stimulate your own intuitive ideas. Struggle in the dark no longer.

- The author has a strong reputation with Tarot enthusiasts
- The first book to fully and exclusively address the interpretation of cards that appear upside-down in a Tarot spread
- Features eleven different methods of determining reversed card meanings
- For readers at all levels of expertise

1-56718-285-2, 6 x 9, 312 pp. $14.95 U.S. $22.95 Can.

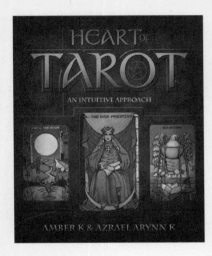